SUFFOLK

A GENEALO
BIBLIOGR.

— BY —

STUART RAY.

FEDERATION OF FAMILY HISTORY SOCIETIES

Published by the
Federation of Family History Societies,
c/o The Benson Room, Birmingham & Midland Institute,
Margaret Street, Birmingham, B3 3BS, U.K.

Copies also available from:
S.A. & M.J. Raymond, 6 Russet Avenue, Exeter, Devon, EX1 3QB, U.K.
S.A. & M.J. Raymond, P.O. Box 255, Belmont, Vic., 3216, Australia.

Text processed and printed by
Oxuniprint, Oxford University Press

Cataloguing in publication data:

RAYMOND, Stuart A., 1945- .
Suffolk: a genealogical bibliography.
British genealogical bibliographies.
Birmingham: Federation of Family History Societies, 1992.

DDC: 016.929094264

ISBN: 1 872094 41 4

ISSN: 1033-2065

CONTENTS

INTRODUCTION

This bibliography is intended primarily for genealogists. It is hoped, however, that it will also prove useful to local historians, librarians, research students, archivists, and anyone else interested in the history of Suffolk and its families. It is designed to be used in conjunction with my *English genealogy: an introductory bibliography* which lists general works relating to the whole of England, and with the other volumes in the *British genealogical bibliographies* series.

Many genealogists fail to appreciate just how much material likely to be of interest to them has been published. Not infrequently, they head for the archives before checking out printed sources first. When faced by the vast array of printed tomes to be found in places such as the three branches of the Suffolk Record Office, they do not know where to begin. This bibliography, in conjunction with others in the series, is intended to point you in the right direction. It is as complete as I have been able to make it. Be warned, however—I make no pretensions to comprehensiveness. Neither do I claim total accuracy. Both these aims are beyond the abilities of any bibliographer. Most items I have seen, but some I have not. Some things I have deliberately excluded; others I have undoubtedly missed. If you come across anything I have missed, please let me know, so that it may be included in a second edition if required. There are innumerable brief notes in journals such as *E.A.M.* and *S.Rt.,* these are not included here unless they include original sources or are otherwise relatively substantial. Replies to such notes, where given, are listed in the form 'see also', with no author's name given.

Unlike most record offices, the three branches of the Suffolk Record Office hold not only the county's archives but also the major collection of published local history. They hold most of the items listed here. Many are also held by libraries throughout the English speaking world—not just in England, but also in North America, Australia and New Zealand. However, some materials, especially journal articles, may be difficult to locate. Never fear! Do not despair of discovering the whereabouts of published genealogical information. Genealogists should expect, indeed, insist, that their local library participate in the international inter-library loan system. Librarians believe, as an article of faith, that all published material should be universally available. Your local library should be able to obtain most of the items listed here, even if it has to go overseas to get them.

The work of compiling this bibliography was undertaken primarily in Exeter, although I also spent time in Ipswich, Bury St.Edmunds, Oxford, Bristol, London and Taunton. The major libraries used were Exeter University Library, Exeter Public Library, Suffolk Record Office, the Bodleian Library, the British Library, the Somerset Archaeological and Natural History Society, Bristol Public Library and Bristol University Library. I am grateful to the librarians of all these libraries for their help. I have also received assistance from Val Andrews of the Somerset and Dorset Family History Society, and from the Cornwall and Devon Family History Societies. My particular thanks go to Dr. Monica Barnett of the Suffolk Family History Society, whose initial encouragement prompted me to target Suffolk, also to Gwyn Thomas, of the Suffolk Record Office, who read the initial typescript. Jeremy Gibson has provided much-needed support. My grateful thanks go to all these people, and also to the officers of the Federation of Family History Societies, whose support is vital to the success of this series.

Stuart A. Raymond

LIBRARIES AND RECORD OFFICES

In Suffolk, local history libraries are administered with the archives, and the three branches of the Suffolk Record Office constitute the major centres for genealogical studies. Their addresses are:

Gatacre Road
IPSWICH
IP1 2LQ

Raingate Street
BURY ST.EDMUNDS
IP33 1RX

Central Library
Clapham Road
LOWESTOFT
NR32 1DR

BIBLIOGRAPHIC PRESENTATION

Authors' names are in SMALL CAPITALS. Book and journal titles are in *italics*. Articles appearing in journals, and material such as parish register transcripts, forming only part of books are in inverted commas and textface type. Volume numbers are in **bold** and the individual number of the journal may be shown in parenthesis. These are normally followed by the place of publication (except where this is London, which is omitted), the name of the publisher and the date of publication. In the case of articles, further figures indicate page numbers.

ABBREVIATIONS

E.A.M.   *East Anglian miscellany*

M.G.H.   *Miscellanea genealogica et heraldica*

N.S.   New series

P.P.R.S.   *Phillimore's parish register series*

R. & B.   *Roots and branches*

S.G.B.   Suffolk Green books

S.I.A.   *Suffolk Institute of Archaeology*

S.P.R.M.   *Suffolk parish registers: marriages*

S.R.S.   Suffolk Records Society

S.Rt.   Suffolk roots

1. THE HISTORY OF SUFFOLK

This bibliography is primarily intended to identify works of immediate value in tracing family trees. However, pure genealogy is of little value unless, through it, we can gain some understanding of the social setting in which our ancestors lived, worked, ate and slept. That understanding will be assisted by the many books available on the history of Suffolk. The following list is only a small selection of some of the best works:

DYMOND, DAVID, & NORTHEAST, PETER. *A history of Suffolk*. Darwen County history, Phillimore, 1985.

RAVEN, JOHN JAMES. *The history of Suffolk*. Elliot Stock, 1895.

WILSON, DEREK. *A short history of Suffolk*. B.T. Batsford, 1977.

Only two general volumes of the *Victoria county history* have so far been published for Suffolk:

PAGE, WILLIAM, ed. *The Victoria history of the county of Suffolk*. Constable & Co., 1907-11. v.1 includes Domesday book; v.2. Ecclesiastical history, school history, etc.

Particular aspects of Suffolk history are dealt with in:

SCARFE, NORMAN. *The Suffolk landscape*. The making of the English landscape. London: Hodder & Stoughton, 1972.

BATES, MARTIN. *East Anglia: Norfolk, Suffolk, Essex, Cambridgeshire*. The Regional Military Histories. Reading: Osprey, 1974.

SCARFE, NORMAN. *Suffolk in the middle ages*. Woodbridge: Boydell Press, 1986.

DOUGLAS, DAVID C. *The social structure of medieval East Anglia*. Oxford studies in social and legal history, **9**. Oxford: Clarendon Press, 1927. Suffolk and Norfolk, 12-13th c.

JOCELIN OF BRAKELOND. *The Chronicle of Jocelin of Brakelond, concerning the acts of Samson, Abbot of the monastery of St.Edmund*, ed. H.E. Buller. Thomas Nelson & Sons, 1949.

GOTTFRIED, ROBERT S. *Bury St.Edmunds and the urban crisis, 1290-1539*. Princeton, N.J.: Princeton U.P., 1982. Includes lists of abbots and aldermen, with a bibliography.

EVANS, NESTA. *The East Anglian linen industry: rural industry and local economy, 1500-1850*. Pasold studies in textile history, **5**. Aldershot: Gower, 1985. Largely based on probate and poor law records.

MACCULLOCH, DIARMAID. *Suffolk and the Tudors: politics and religion in an English county, 1500-1600*. Oxford: Clarendon Press, 1986.

SIMPSON, ALAN. *The wealth of the gentry, 1540-1660: East Anglian studies*. Cambridge: C.U.P., 1961. Studies of Sir Nicholas Bacon, Sir Thomas Cullum and Sir Thomas Cornwallis.

MACCULLOCH, DIARMAID. 'The impact of the reformation on Suffolk parish life', *Suffolk review*, N.S. **15**, 1990, 1-19.

BLACKWOOD, B. GORDON. 'The cavalier and roundhead gentry of Suffolk', *Suffolk review*, N.S. **5**, 1985, 1-10, and **7**, 1986, 1-8.

BLACKWOOD, B. GORDON. 'The marriages of the cavalier and roundhead gentry of Suffolk', *Genealogists magazine* **22**(4), 1986, 136-9.

HOLMES, CLIVE. *The Eastern Association in the English Civil War*. Cambridge: C.U.P., 1974.

JOBSON, ALLAN. *Victorian Suffolk*. Robert Hale, 1972. Just one of many Suffolk titles by a popular author.

EVANS, GEORGE EWART. *Ask the fellows who cut the hay*. Faber & Faber, 1956. A study of 'pre-machine village life in Suffolk', based on Blaxhall.

GLIDDON, GERALD, ed. *Norfolk and Suffolk in the Great War*. Norwich: Gliddon Books, 1988.

BLYTHE, RONALD. *Akenfield: portrait of an English village*. Allen Lane, 1969. Description of a pseudonymous village—actually Chasfield—in the 1950s.

The historical uses of sources used by genealogists are illustrated in a number of articles:

GRACE, F.R. 'The population of East Bergholt, 1653-1836: an analysis of the parish registers', *Suffolk review* **3**, 1970, 260-72.

LAVROVSKY, V.M. 'Parliamentary enclosures in the county of Suffolk (1797-1814)', *Economic history review* **7**(2), 1937, 186-208.

OVERTON, MARK. 'Estimating crop yields from probate inventories: an example from East Anglia', *Journal of Economic history* **39**, 1979, 363-78. Norfolk and Suffolk.

PATTEN, JOHN. 'Village and town: an occupational study', *Agricultural history review* **20**, 1972, 1-16. Study of the muster rolls of Babergh Hundred, 1522.

Older histories are frequently more useful to genealogists, since they often contain many pedigrees and extracts from genealogical sources such as parish registers, monumental inscriptions, wills, etc. Of particular value are those works which survey the parochial history of the county. The oldest such work, compiled c.1600-5, although not published until 1976, is:

MACCULLOCH, DIARMAID, ed. *The chorography of Suffolk.* S.R.S., **19**. Ipswich: Boydell Press, 1976.

Another seventeenth-century description of the county, which includes notes on many families, with pedigrees of Wingfield and Waldegrave, is:

REYCE, ROBERT. *Suffolk in the XVIIth century: being the breviary of Suffolk,* ed. Lord Francis Hervey. John Murray, 1902.

Other parochial surveys include:

A compleat history of Suffolk ... T. Cox, 1730.

SUCKLING, ALFRED. *The history and antiquities of the county of Suffolk, with genealogical and architectural notices of its several towns and villages.* 2 vols. John Weale, 1846-8. Includes many pedigrees. A separate index volume was published Ipswich: W.S. Cowell, 1952.

PAGE, AUGUSTINE. *A supplement to the Suffolk traveller, or, topographical and genealogical collections concerning that county.* Ipswich: Joshua Page; London: J.B. Nichols & Son, 1844.

PAGE, AUGUSTINE. *Topographical and genealogical history of the county of Suffolk. Compiled from authentic records.* Ipswich: F. Pawsey, 1847.

BARKER, H.R. *East Suffolk illustrated.* Bury St.Edmunds: F.G. Pawsey & Co., 1908-9.

BARKER, H.R. *West Suffolk illustrated.* Bury St.Edmunds: F.G. Pawsey & Co., 1907.

A parochial survey for Thingoe Hundred, with lists of incumbents, pedigrees, etc., is:

GAGE, JOHN. *The history and antiquities of Suffolk: Thingoe, Hundred.* John Deak, 1838.

A number of antiquaries attempted to collect source material for the history of Suffolk. A detailed index to sources, both published and manuscript, in the Public Record Office, the British Library, etc., is provided by:

COPINGER, WALTER A. *County of Suffolk: its history as disclosed by existing records and other documents, being materials for the history of Suffolk* ... 5 vols. Henry Sotheran & Co., 1904-5. This is indexed in:

COPINGER, H.B. *Index nominum et locorum, being an index of names of persons and places mentioned in Copinger's County of Suffolk* ... Manchester: privately printed, 1907.

Another monumental work—which is also monumentally incompetent, but must nevertheless be used—is:

COPINGER, WALTER ARTHUR. *The manors of Suffolk: notes on their history and devolution.* 7 vols. T. Fisher Unwin, 1905-11. This may be supplemented by MacCulloch's edition of the *Chorography*, noted above, for descents of manors.

Many deeds, wills, pedigrees, etc., are printed in:

ALDRED, HENRY W., ed. *The Suffolk records.* Elliot Stock, 1888. Issued in parts.

The activities of a nineteenth century antiquary, whose collection is now in the British Library (see Section 2) are chronicled in:

DAVY, DAVID ELISHA. *A journal of excursions through the county of Suffolk, 1823-1844.* ed. John Blatchly. S.R.S., **24**. Woodbridge: Boydell Press, 1982.

2. BIBLIOGRAPHY AND ARCHIVES

The present work is devoted to Suffolk genealogy. If you want to know more about historical publications on Suffolk—and you will almost certainly want to see some of the many parochial histories which are excluded here—consult:

STEWARD, A.V. *A Suffolk bibliography*. S.R.S., **20**, 1979. This gives locations for the rarer titles.

A briefer bibliography, but with much more detailed annotations, is provided by:

Suffolk local history: a short bibliography. Ipswich: Suffolk Local History Council, 1970.

An older work is:

McCOLVIN, L.R. *Suffolk: a list of books* 2nd ed. [National Book Council], 1929.

For current publications, see:

East Anglian bibliography: a checklist of publications not in the British National Bibliography. Library Association (Eastern Branch), 1960-

If you live in East Anglia, and want to locate some of the works listed here, consult:

HUMPHREY, ELIZABETH. *Periodicals and sets relating to British history in Norfolk and Suffolk libraries: a finding list*. University of East Anglia Centre of East Anglian Studies, [1970]. Includes listings of poll books, parish magazines, local society publications, directories, etc., as well as national publications.

A useful guide to local libraries is provided by:

HUMPHREY, ELIZABETH. *History collections in Norfolk and Suffolk libraries: a handbook*. Norwich: University of East Anglia Library, [1970].

For the important library of the Suffolk Institute of Archaeology (now housed by the Bury St.Edmunds branch of Suffolk Record Office), see:

SUFFOLK INSTITUTE OF ARCHAEOLOGY AND NATURAL HISTORY. *Catalogue of books in the library at the Athenaeum, Bury St.Edmunds*. Bury St.Edmunds: the Institute, 1933.

Another antiquarian collection is catalogued in:

BARKER, H.R. *Moyses Hall Museum, Bury St.Edmunds: catalogue of the printed books, pamphlets and miscellaneous papers*. Bury St.Edmunds: the Museum, 1903.

Many local family histories are listed in:

STEDMAN, A.E. 'Index to family and personal histories relating to East Anglia in the 'Indexes to Archaeological Papers', 1891-1905', *East Anglian* N.S. **12**,1907-8, 53-4; N.S. **13**, 1909-10, 87.

Agricultural history may not seem to be immediately relevant to the genealogist. Nevertheless, if you want to identify works which will help you acquire the 'flavour' of the county, see:

DYMOND, DAVID, PAINE, CLIVE & PLACE, MONICA. *Suffolk agriculture: a critical bibliography*. Ipswich: Suffolk Record Office, 1978.

Theses in general are almost totally ignored by genealogists. Yet some could provide useful clues. For a list, see:

BAKER, GILLIAN. *East Anglian history: theses completed*. Norwich: University of East Anglia Centre of East Anglian Studies, 1972.

HENNEY, JANICE. *East Anglian studies: theses completed*. Norwich: Centre of East Anglian Studies, 1982.

The Suffolk Record Office, with its branches at Ipswich, Bury St.Edmunds and Lowestoft, is the major Suffolk archive repository. A now rather out of date description of its Ipswich holdings is given in:

CHARMAN, DEREK. 'Local archives of Great Britain, XVII: The Ipswich and East Suffolk Record Office', *Archives* **4**(21), 1959, 18-28.

Lists of parish registers and census microfilm, together with a brief description of probate records, are provided by:

SUFFOLK RECORD OFFICE. *Guide to genealogical sources*. 3rd ed. Ipswich: Suffolk County Council, 1987.

For accessions to the record office, reference should be made to:

Ipswich and East Suffolk Record Office: Annual report of the Joint Archivist ... Ipswich: the Office, 1953-72. Reports cover 1952-3, 1953-4, 1954-5, 1955-6 and 1970-2.

Suffolk Record Office ... report. Ipswich: the Office, 1979-83. Reports cover 1974-9, 1979-80, 1980-82 and 1982-3.

Suffolk Record Office annual report. [Ipswich]: the Office, 1983-. Roneod; includes new accessions until 1988.

See also:

Archive news: the newsletter of the Suffolk Record Office. Ipswich: Suffolk Record Office, 1973-83. Amongst other useful information, provides listings of new accessions. Originally published Ipswich: East Suffolk Record Office. The second series (same title) commenced 1989-

'Bury St.Edmunds and West Suffolk records: recent acquisitions', *Suffolk review* **3**(1), 1965-70, 34-5; **3**(2), 1965-70, 23 and 96-7.

Bibliography and Archives *continued*

Various collections of the Suffolk Record Office are listed in:

'Suffolk county records', *S.I.A.* **15**, 1915, 144-51.

SONI, SUSHIL K. 'Suffolk and India', *Suffolk review* **6**, 1986, 15-26. Includes a list of archives at Suffolk Record Office.

REDSTONE, LILIAN J. 'Inventory of the records deposited by the Suffolk Institute of Archaeology at the Ipswich Public Library', *S.I.A.* **23**, 1939, 187-201. Mainly deeds and other estate papers.

Suffolk manuscripts at the British Library are listed in a number of works:

BULLEN, R.F. 'Suffolk manuscripts in the British Library', *E.A.M.* **1913**, 87-8 and 92-3. Listed by parish and family.

GRAY, GEORGE J. *Index to the contents of the Cole manuscripts in the British Museum.* Cambridge: Bowes & Bowes, 1912. Lists an antiquarian collection which includes many original sources for Suffolk, although primarily of Cambridgeshire interest.

LEVIEN, E. 'On ms. collections relating to Suffolk in the British Museum.' *Journal of the British Archaeological Association* **21**, 1865, 5-21. Includes notes on many items of genealogical interest, including a volume of wills and deeds.

SANDERSON, ROUNDELL P. 'The topography of Suffolk: references to mss. in the British Museum', *East Anglian* N.S. **4**, 1891-2, 183-5 and 262-6; N.S. **5**, 1893-4, 361.

The important Davy collection at the British Library is listed in a number of works:

GATFIELD, GEO. 'Index to Davy's Suffolk collections', *Genealogist,* N.S. **5**, 1888, 117-28; **6**, 1890, 56-63, 108-15, 139-45 and 250-51.

COPINGER, W.A. 'Davy's Suffolk collections, British Museum, Additional Mss. 19172', *East Anglian* N.S. **8**, 1899-1900, 373-6; **9**, 1901-2, 9-12, 21-3, 56-8, 70-2 and 88-9. See also **9**, 1901-2, 12-14 and 156; **12**,1907-8, 161-2.

'Davy's Suffolk collections', *S.I.A.* **6**, 1888, 437-55. Includes many extracts from deeds, etc., with monumental inscriptions, notes on ministers, and parish register extracts.

A number of other antiquarian collections have been listed:

FITCH, WILLIAM STEVENSON. *Catalogue of manorial registers, royal grants and deeds, court-baron, leet and rent rolls, surveys, letters, papers, seals, engravings, drawings, autographs and other authentic documents, collected for the purpose of illustrating a history of the county ...* Great Yarmouth: C. Sloman, 1843.

FARRER, EDMUND. 'The Dunthorne mss.', *S.I.A.* **20**, 1930, 147-85. Description of an antiquarian collection of notes concerning Dennington in particular, and Suffolk in general. Includes pedigree of Green and Dunthorne, 18-19th c.

KING, T.W. 'Collection of mss. in Coll. Arm. for Co.Suffolk', *Journal of the British Archaeological Association* **21**, 1865, 158-9.

CAMP, ANTHONY J. 'The Campling collection for Norfolk and Suffolk', *Family tree magazine* **2**(1), 1985, 17. Describes collection of genealogical notes at the Society of Genealogists.

A useful note on tax lists, court rolls, parish registers, etc., in Colneis Hundred is provided by:

TOLLIDAY, DAVID. 'Sources for research into the population of the Colneis Hundred', *R. & B.* **2**(1), 1987, 12-13.

3. JOURNALS AND NEWSPAPERS

The most important journal for genealogists in Suffolk is:

Suffolk roots: the journal of the Suffolk Genealogy Society. Lowestoft: the Society, 1975-. The first 3 issues had no title. Sub-titled *The journal of the Suffolk Family History Society* from 14(3)-, 1988-.

For Felixstowe, see also:

Roots and branches: Journal of the Felixstowe Family History Society. 1986-.

Both these journals carry extensive information relating to the interests of their members, and thus enable you to contact others who may be researching your own lines.

For Suffolk heraldry, consult:

The Blazon: newletter of the Suffolk Heraldry Society. The Society, 1977-.

Many original sources—mostly listed in the appropriate sections below—have been published in:

Suffolk Records Society publications. Ipswich: the Society, 1958-.

Newspapers are an important source of genealogical information—especially their births, marriages and deaths columns. Suffolk newspapers are listed in:

GORDON, RUTH. *Newsplan: report of the Newsplan project in the East Midlands, April 1987-July 1988.* British Library, 1989.

The most substantial historical journal for Suffolk is:

Proceedings of the Suffolk Institute of Archaeology and History ... Bury St.Edmunds: the Society, 1853-. Title varies. 1st issue entitled *Proceedings of the Bury and West Suffolk Archaeological Institute* ...

This is indexed in:

DOW, LESLIE. 'Indexes to *Proceedings,* vols.I-XXIV (1848-1948)', *S.I.A.* **24**, 1949, 144-60.

'Index to articles, *Proceedings,* vols.XXV-XXX (1949-1966)', *S.I.A.* **30**, 1967, 306-8.

Also important is:

Suffolk Local History Council Bulletin. Ipswich: the Council, 1953-6.

Continued as:

The Suffolk review. Ipswich: Suffolk Local History Council, 1958-.

If you want to know what is currently happening in Suffolk local history, consult:

Suffolk local history newsletter. Ipswich: Suffolk Local History Council, 1969-.

Suffolk archaeology and history newsletter. Suffolk Institute of Archaeology, 1975-.

Two valuable local journals are:

Haverhill historian: journal of the Haverhill and District Local History Group. Haverhill: the Group, 1977-.

Pagus: a quarterly magazine of the Barrow and District Local History Society. Barrow: the Society, 1983-88. Originally bi-monthly.

Many miscellaneous notes and queries on genealogical topics, some of which are noted below, are included in:

East Anglian miscellany upon matters of history, genealogy, archaeology, folk-lore, literature, etc., relating to East Anglia. Ipswich: East Anglian Daily Times, 1907-58. An index is provided in each annual volume; a typescript index is available at the Ipswich and Bury St.Edmunds branches of Suffolk Record Office.

Similar, if somewhat more substantial, material is included in:

The East Anglian, or, notes and queries on subjects connected with the counties of Suffolk, Cambridge, Essex and Norfolk. 4 + 13 vols. Lowestoft: S.Tymms; London: Whitaker & Co., 1858-71. New series, 1885-1910. Each volume has its own index to persons, places and subjects, except that only subjects are indexed from N.S. 7-.

The gap in publication of the *East Anglian* between 1871 and 1885 was partly filled by:

L'ESTRANGE, JOHN. *Eastern Counties Collectanea, being notes and queries on subjects relating to the counties of Norfolk, Suffolk, Essex and Cambridge.* Norwich: Thomas R. Tallack, 1872-3. This is sometimes referred to as v.5 of the *East Anglian.*

Of lesser importance, but with a good index, is:

East Anglian Magazine. Ipswich: East Anglian Magazine, 1935-.

This is indexed in:

MOLLARD, T. *Index to the East Anglian Magazine, July 1935 (issue no.1) to December 1960.* Ipswich: Library Association (Eastern Branch), 1968.

Parish magazines form a potentially useful source. A general discussion of their value, together with some examples from Frostenden, may be found in:

SCRIVEN, PAUL. 'The parish magazine: a neglected source', *Suffolk review,* N.S. **3**, 1984, 3-9.

Finally, a word of warning: despite the sub-title, the following has little of relevance to Suffolk, although it is useful for East Anglia generally:

Fenland notes and queries: a quarterly antiquarian journal for the counties of Huntingdon, Cambridge, Lincoln, Northampton, Norfolk and Suffolk. 7 vols. Peterborough: [ ], 1889-1909.

4. NAMES AND DIALECT

Obscure place-names frequently occur in genealogical sources, and an adequate place-name dictionary is needed to identify them. Unfortunately, Suffolk has not yet been treated by the English Place Name Society's survey. Reference may, however, be made to:

SKEAT, WALTER W. *The place-names of Suffolk*. Publications: Octavo Series, **46**. Cambridge: Deighton Bell & Co. for the Cambridge Antiquarian Society, 1913. From an etymological point of view, this work has dubious value.

A more up to date listing of minor place names is provided by:

MARTIN, EDWARD A. *Suffolk minor place-names: an annotated list*. 1985. Typescript.

For place-names of the Deben Valley parishes, see:

ARNOTT, W.G. *The place-names of the Deben Valley parishes*. Ipswich: Norman Adland & Co., 1946.

The origin of East Anglian surnames has been treated fully, and much valuable information is contained in:

McKINLEY, RICHARD. *Norfolk and Suffolk surnames in the middle ages*. English surnames series, **2**. Phillimore, 1975.

On modern nicknames, see:

VALIANT, F.A. & ANDREWS, L.E. 'Nicknames of Barrow', *Pagus* **8**, 1984, 8-11. Includes list, e.g. 'Gunboat Smith' from c.1920-50.

Dialect words may also appear in genealogical sources. For their meaning, consult one of the following:

CLAXTON, A.O.D. *The Suffolk dialect of the 20th century*. 3rd ed. Woodbridge: Boydell Press, 1968.

FORBY, ROBERT. *The vocabulary of East Anglia*. 2 vols. Newton Abbot: David & Charles, 1970. Originally published J.B.Nichols & Son, 1830.

MOOR, EDWARD. *Suffolk words and phrases*. Newton Abbot: David & Charles, 1970. Originally published R.Hunter, 1823.

RYE, WALTER. *Glossary of words used in East Anglia, founded on that of Forby*. English Dialect Society, 1895.

5. PEDIGREE COLLECTIONS AND HERALDRY

In the sixteenth and seventeenth centuries, the heralds undertook 'visitations' of the counties in order to determine the right of gentry to bear heraldic arms. One consequence of this activity was the compilation of pedigrees of most of the leading gentry. These visitation pedigrees continue to be major sources of genealogical information, and many have been published— although few editions meet the standard set by:

CORDER, JOAN, ed. *The visitation of Suffolk 1561, made by William Hervy*. Publications of the Harleian Society, N.S. **2-3**, 1981-4. This includes many references to other sources of information.

Other published visitation returns include:

HOWARD, JOSEPH JACKSON, ed. *The visitation of Suffolke, made by William Hervey, Clarenceux King of Armes, 1561, with additions from family documents, original wills, Jermyn, Davy and other mss., etc.* 2 vols. Lowestoft: Samuel Tymms, 1866-76. Includes many wills, extracts from parish registers, monumental inscriptions, etc.

METCALFE, WALTER C., ed. *The visitations of Suffolk made by Hervey, Clarenceux, 1561; Cooke, Clarenceux, 1577; and Raven, Richmond Herald, 1612, with notes and an appendix of additional Suffolk pedigrees*. Exeter: William Pollard, 1882.

RYLANDS, W. HARRY, ed. *A visitation of the county of Suffolk, begun anno dni. 1662, finished anno dni. 1668, by Sir Edward Bysshe, Kt., Clarenceux King of Arms*. Publications of the Harleian Society, **61**, 1910.

Surviving visitation families are listed in:

SAYER, M.J. 'Surviving Norfolk and Suffolk visitation families', *Genealogists magazine* **18**, 1975-6, 343-7. See also **19**, 1977-8, 20.

Other collections of pedigrees include:

CAMPLING, ARTHUR, ed. *East Anglian pedigrees*. Norfolk Record Society, **13**, 1940. Includes many Suffolk pedigrees; excludes, for the most part, pedigrees of families in the visitation returns.

MUSKETT, J.J., ed. *Suffolk manorial families, being the county visitation and other pedigrees*. 3 vols. Exeter: William Pollard & Co., 1900-14. Includes many wills, monumental inscriptions, etc.

[CRISP, F.A., ed.] *Fragmenta genealogica, vol.IX*. F.A.Crisp, 1903. This volume consists of East Anglian pedigrees, primarily Norfolk and Suffolk.

Pedigrees of many Bildeston families are included in:

GROWSE, FREDERICK SALMON. *Materials for a history of the parish of Bildeston ... with pedigrees and genealogical notices of the families of Alston, Barker, Beaumont, Blomfield, Brand, Cooke, Cole, Edge, Growse, Johnson, Loveyn, Parker, Parsons, Revett, Salmon, Stebbing, Terry, Wade, Wilson, compiled in the year 1859, revised and brought up to date in 1891.* Privately printed, 1892. This also includes a list of rectors, deed abstracts, etc.

Lists of manuscript pedigrees are provided by:

FARRER, EDMUND. 'The Blois mss.', *S.I.A.* **14**, 1912, 147-226. Discussion of mss. volumes of pedigrees and church notes, etc., in the possession of the Suffolk Institute; provides an index to the pedigrees and church notes, and prints the armory.

'Pedigrees of Suffolk families', *East Anglian* **4**, 1870, passim; N.S. **1-3**, 1885/6-1889/90, passim. Lists pedigrees in the Davy manuscripts at the British Library.

Heraldry is a useful adjunct to genealogical studies. A general guide to Suffolk heraldry is provided by:

CORDER, JOAN. *A dictionary of Suffolk arms.* S.R.S., **7**, 1965.

See also:

DOW, L. 'A Suffolk heraldic manuscript', *S.I.A.* **25**, 1952, 288-96. Description of a 17th c. ms. giving many coats of arms. Includes biographical notes on many Suffolk antiquaries.

FARRER, EDMUND. 'Early Suffolk heraldry', *S.I.A.* **21**, 1933, 1-52. Heraldic notes on 91 armorial seals.

WHAYMAN, HORACE W. 'The antient and modern nobility in Suffolk', *East Anglian* N.S. **7**, 1897-8, 24-9, 44-8, 59-62, 82-5, 113-7, 150-2, 228-30 and 251-2. See also N.S. **6**, 1895-6, 251-5, for index. Transcript of an armorial, c.1800.

'A Suffolk armory', *Family history* **1**(3), 1963, 82-96; **1**(4), 1964, 101-11; **1**(5), 1963, 133-6. Compiled c.1596-1606.

'Suffolk arms circa 1605', *M.G.H.* 5th series, **6**, 1926-8, 11-15.

For other works on heraldy, see Section 9.

6. BIOGRAPHICAL DICTIONARIES, GENEALOGICAL DIRECTORIES AND OCCUPATIONAL LISTS

One of the most valuable sources of current genealogical information are the directories of interests published by family history societies. These provide the names and addresses of researchers, together with the names of families they are researching. If your surname is listed, maybe much of the work on your line has been completed! Or at least there may be someone willing to share the work. For Suffolk, see:

1991 handbook: lists of the membership and their interests. [ ]: Suffolk F.H.S., 1991.

Biographical dictionaries provide brief biographical information on the individuals listed. Innumerable such dictionaries exist, and are invaluable to the genealogist. To identify them, consult the sources listed in my *English genealogy: an introductory bibliography.* Suffolk biographical dictionaries include:

HASLEWOOD, FRANCIS. 'The ancient families of Suffolk', *S.I.A.* **8**, 1894, 121-214.

LANGHAM, GEORGE H. *Eminent East Anglians.* Cassell, 1904.

PIKE, W.T. *East Anglia in the twentieth century—contemporary biographies.* Brighton: W.T. Pike & Co., 1912. Suffolk and Norfolk.

PIKE, W.T. & HUSSEY. F. *Norfolk and Suffolk in East Anglia: contemporary biographies.* Brighton: W.T. Pike, 1911.

PRESS, C.A. MANNING. *Suffolk celebrities.* Leeds: McConquodale, 1893. 44 biographies.

PRESS, C.A. MANNING. *Suffolk leaders: social and political.* Horney & Tottenham Press, 1906.

SMITH-DAMPIER, J.L. *East Anglian worthies.* Oxford: Basil Blackwell, 1949. 200 biographical sketches, Suffolk and Norfolk.

Cox's county who's who series: Norfolk, Suffolk and Cambridgeshire, 1912. Horace Cox, 1912.

Public men of Ipswich and East Suffolk: a series of personal sketches. Ipswich: W.J. Scopes, 1875. 45 brief biographies.

Who's who in Suffolk. Worcester: Ebenezer Baylis & Son, 1935.

For Ipswich, see:

CLARKE, G.R. *History and description of the town and borough of Ipswich, including the villages and country seats in its vicinity ...* Ipswich: S.Piper, 1830. Includes 'biographical catalogue of distinguished personages connected with ... Ipswich', and lists of recorders, bailiffs, etc.

Who's who in Ipswich. Pullman Press, 1959.

Biographical Dictionaries etc. *continued*

Whilst not strictly biographical dictionaries, the following two works do provide useful biographical information:

BLATCHLY, JOHN. *Eighty Ipswich portraits: Samuel Read's early Victorian sketchbook*. Ipswich: John Blatchly, 1980.

FARRER, EDMUND. *Portraits in Suffolk houses (West)*. Bernard Quaritch, 1908. Lists portraits, with some biographical information on those portrayed.

There are many works offering biographical information on persons with a particular occupation or status. These are listed here. For clergymen, see section 13; for local government officers, section 16 This list may be supplemented by the national sources listed in my *Occupational sources for genealogists*.

Apothecaries

WHITTET, T. DOUGLAS. 'Suffolk apothecaries' tokens and their issuers', *Suffolk review*, N.S. **9**, 1987, 19-35. Includes biographical notes on 17th c. issuers.

ZWANENBURG, D. VAN. 'The training and careers of those apprenticed to apothecaries in Suffolk, 1815-1858', *Medical history* **27**, 1983, 139-50. General discussion.

Apprentices

'Suffolk apprentices on the books of the Carpenters Company, London, 1655-93', *E.A.M.* 1917, 64-5 and 66-7.

See also Apothecaries and Sailors

Architects

BROWN, CYNTHIA; HAWARD, BIRKIN & KINDRED, ROBERT. *Dictionary of architects of Suffolk buildings, 1800-1914*. Ipswich: Brown Haward & Kindred, 1991.

Bankers

JONES, A.G.E. 'Early banking in Bury St.Edmunds', *Notes and queries* **199**, 1954, 169-73, 209-12 and 265-6. Gives many names of bankers.

JONES, A.G.E. 'Early banking in Suffolk', *Notes and queries* **199**, 1954, 438-40 and 482-4; **200**, 1954, 28-30, 78-80, 170-73 and 398-401. See also 313. Gives many names.

Bankrupts

JONES, A.G.E. 'Suffolk bankruptcies in the 18th century', *Suffolk review* **2**(1), 1951, 4-10. See also N.S. **2**, 1984, 7-10. General discussion of sources.

Bellfounders

MANDER, R.P. 'Medieval bell-founders of Norfolk and Suffolk', *East Anglian Magazine* **8**, 1949, 665-70. Brief note.

Booksellers

BULLEN, R. FREEMAN. 'Suffolk booksellers in the 18th century', *E.A.M.* **1910**, 64. Gives names, places and dates.

Book Subscribers

H., L.J. 'East Anglian list, 1737', *E.A.M.* **1919**, 1, 4, 6, 8, 10, 14, 15-16, 18, 20-21, 22-3, 24, 29-30, 32, 33-4, 36 and 37-8. See also p.54. List of subscribers to a book, from Norfolk and Suffolk.

Brewers

BRISTOW, C.R. *A directory of nineteenth and twentieth century Suffolk brewers*. Ipswich: Salient Press, 1985. Includes much biographical information on brewers.

Carpenters

See Apprentices

Clockmakers

HAGGAR, ARTHUR L. & MILLER, LEONARD F. *Suffolk clocks and clockmakers*. Wadhurst: Antiquarian Horological Society, 1974. Includes list of makers, with biographical notes.

Freemasons

BENTHAM, R. *History of the Doric Lodge, No.81, Woodbridge, 1824-1923*. Woodbridge: George Booth, 1932. Includes full list of members, plus many extracts from minutes etc., giving names.

SADD, A. HAROLD & MARTIN, L.J. *The minute books of British Union Lodge, No.114, Ipswich, part 1: 1762 to 1874*. Ipswich: W.E. Harrison & Sons, 1932. Includes lists of masters, and of members in 1932. Many other names appear in the minutes, but unfortunately there is no index.

WATSON, S.F. *History of Victorian Chapter of S.P. Rose Croix of H.R.D.M., No.22, Ipswich, 1867-1967*. Ipswich: Browns, 1967. Gives many names.

WATSON, S.F. *A history of British Union Lodge, No.114, Ipswich, 1762-1962*. Ipswich: W.S. Cowell, 1962. Includes list of members giving occupations, residences, ages, etc.

Innkeepers

THOMPSON, LEONARD P. *Old inns of Suffolk*. Ipswich: W.E. Harrison & Sons, 1946. Gives names of many innkeepers, and notes on their inns.

Master Mariners
See Sailors

Medics
TYMMS, SAMUEL. 'Notes towards a medical history of Bury', *Proceedings of the Bury and West Suffolk Archaeological Institute* 1, 1853, 33-49. Includes biographical notes on medics.

VERTUE, F.H. 'List of medical men living in 1728, residing in Cambridge, Suffolk, and Norfolk', *East Anglian* N.S. 2, 1887-8, 10-11.

Millwrights
WAILES, REX. 'Suffolk watermills', *Newcomen Society ... Transactions* 37, 1964-5, 99-116. Includes list of millwrights, etc.

Painters
BENNETT, CHLOE. *Suffolk artists, 1750-1920.* Woolpit: Imager Publications, 1991.

DAY, HAROLD A.E. *East Anglian painters.* 3 vols. Eastbourne: Eastbourne Fine Art, 1968-9. Includes biographical notes. Covers Essex, Suffolk and Norfolk.

Pipemakers
OAK-RHIND, H.H. 'Clay tobacco pipe makers of Suffolk', *Suffolk review* 4(4), 1975, 195-211. Includes list with brief biographical notes.

Printers
WATSON, S.F. 'Some materials for a history of printing and publishing in Ipswich', *S.I.A.* 24, 1949, 182-227. Gives brief accounts of many printers.

Sailors
REDSTONE, V.B. 'Ipswich port books', *S.I.A.* 14, 1912, 238-42. Gives names of masters of ships arriving at and departing from Ipswich, 1634-5.

STANNARD, E. 'List of Southwold ships', *S.Rt.* 5(2), 1978, 20; 5(3), 1979, 50; 5(4), 1979, 60; 6(1), 1980, 11; 6(2), 1980, 28. Lists ships and masters, late 18th-early 19th c.

WEBB, JOHN. 'Apprenticeships in the maritime occupations at Ipswich, 1590-1651', *Mariner's Mirror* 46, 1960, 29-34. Discussion of a book containing official enrolments of apprenticeships.

'Ipswich master mariners', *E.A.M.* 1952, passim. Includes detailed biographical notes.

Servants
'Shropham and Guiltcross Association awards, 1836', *Pagus* 20, 1987, 17-22. Lists many winners of prizes awarded to servants, labourers, etc.

Shipbuilders
JONES, A.G.E. 'Shipbuilding in Ipswich, 1700-1750', *Mariner's Mirror* 43, 1957, 294-305. Continued for the period 1750-1800 in 58, 1972, 183-93. Gives some names.

Shipowners
MOFFAT, HUGH. 'The Woodbridge shipping register', *Suffolk review* 6, 1986, 1-4. Describes a source of information on shipowners.

Ship's Masters
See Sailors

Soldiers, Militiamen and Volunteers
Many men of Suffolk served in the army or the militia, and much information on them is available in the various regimental histories, honour rolls, etc., which have been published. These cannot all be listed here. The following works all include lists of names or other information of direct genealogical value. General histories with no information of use to genealogists are excluded.

DAVIES, GODFREY. 'The army of the Eastern Association, 1644-5', *English historical review* 46, 1931, 88-96. Includes list of Parliamentary officers.

M., R.W. 'The hair of Suffolk soldiers, 1624', *E.A.M.* 1911, 21-2. List of men pressed in Ipswich for service in the Palatinate, giving ages and descriptions—including the colour of their hair!

WEBB, E.A.H. *History of the 12th (the Suffolk) Regiment, 1685-1913. Including a brief history of the East and West Suffolk Militia, the latter being now the 3rd Battalion, Suffolk Regiment.* Spottiswoode & Co., 1914. Includes lists of colonels and lieutenant colonels, etc., with many other names.

'Suffolk recruits for Marlborough's army', *E.A.M.* 1935, 85, 88, 90 and 91; 1936, passim. Militia list, 1704, lists recruits by district.

P[ARTRIDGE], C., & M., S.M.W. 'Soldiers at Hadleigh, 1754-1812', *E.A.M.* 1941, 28.

'The Suffolk militia in 1759', *E.A.M.* 1913, 37-8. Lists commissioned officers and captains.

WYATT, R.J. 'Suffolk volunteers at Worlingworth, 1798-1802', *Journal of the Society for Army Historical Research* 61, 1983, 92-5. Discussion of potential sources for Volunteer history.

PYATT, EILEEN. '12th Foot: East Suffolk Regiment', *S.Rt.* 7(1), 1981, 11-14. Index of Suffolk born men who joined the regiment, 1800-1827.

Soldiers, Militiamen and Volunteers *continued*

BUNT, EILEEN. 'Did your ancestor join the 'Company' army?', *S.Rt.* **12**(3), 1986, 67-8. List of Suffolk soldiers of the East India Company, 1816-22.

FAIR, A. & WOLTON, E.D. *The history of the 1/5th Battalion, the Suffolk Regiment.* Eyre & Spottiswoode, [1923]. Covers 1859-1921; includes roll of honour.

SLACK, JAMES. *The history of the late 73rd (West Suffolk) Regiment.* Army & Navy Co-operative Society, 1884. Includes much biographical information on Colonels.

MURPHY, C.C.R. *The history of the Suffolk Regiment, 1914-27.* Hutchinson & Co., 1928. Includes many names.

CHRISTIE, PETER. 'Oddments from the archives, 25', *S.Rt.* **9**(2), 1983, 36-7. Lists 86 Exning villagers killed in the First World War.

'In St.Margaret's Church, Lowestoft, during 1914-1918 war', *S.Rt.* **9**(4), 1983, 82-3. List of men serving in the armed forces.

Soldiers died in the Great War, 1914-19. Pt.17: the Suffolk Regiment. H.M.S.O., 1921. Reprinted Chippenham: Picton, 1988. List with brief biographical notes.

A memorial service for officers, warrant officers, non-commissioned officers, and men from Suffolk who have fallen in the War. Ipswich: W.E. Harrison, 1919. Includes roll of honour of the fallen.

COMMONWEALTH WAR GRAVES COMMISSION. *The war graves of the British Empire: the register of the names of those who fell in the Great War and are buried in cemeteries and churchyards in ... East and West Suffolk.* The Commission, 1931.

NICHOLSON, W.M. *The Suffolk Regiment, 1928-46.* Ipswich, East Anglian Magazine, [1948]. Includes many names.

IMPERIAL WAR GRAVES COMMISSION. *The war dead of the Commonwealth: the register of the names of those who fell in the 1939-1945 War and are buried in cemeteries and churchyards in the county of Suffolk.* The Commission, 1961. Reprinted with amendments, 1988.

GODFREY, F.A. *The history of the Suffolk Regiment, 1946-1959.* Leo Cooper, 1988. Includes various lists of officers, etc.

Swan Owners

TICEHURST, N.F. 'The swan-marks of Suffolk', *S.I.A.* **21**, 1933, 139-52. Includes list of owners of swans, 16-17th c., with brief biographical notes.

Topographers

BLATCHLY, JOHN. *The topographers of Suffolk, 1561-1935: brief biographies and specimens of the hands of selected Suffolk antiquaries.* 5th ed. Ipswich: Suffolk Record Office, 1988. Includes much bibliographic information as well as the biographies.

Traders

In an age when coinage was in short supply, many traders issued their own tokens. Studies of these tokens often provide information of genealogical value. For Suffolk, see:

GOLDING, CHARLES. *The coinage of Suffolk, consisting of the regal coins, leaden pieces and tokens of the seventeenth, eighteenth and nineteenth centuries, together with notices of the mints and of some of the issuers of tokens.* J.E. Taylor & Co., 1868.

This is corrected in:

CRANBROOK, EARL OF. 'Notes on some new and doubtful 17th century Suffolk tokens', *S.I.A.* **24**, 1949, 63-99. Listed by place of origin, with many names of traders.

Winesellers

M., R.W. 'Suffolk winesellers in 1625', *E.A.M.* **1910**, 123-4. List.

7. FAMILY HISTORIES, PEDIGREES, ETC.

Works relating to the history of particular families are listed here. Biographies, however, are not included. For them, reference should be made to Steward's *Suffolk bibliography*. (See above, 9)

Abbot

'Suffolk pedigrees', *M.G.H.* 5th series, **9**, 1935-7, 12-14. Includes Abbot of Sudbury, 17-18th c., and Acton of Baylham, 17-19th c.

Acton

See Abbot

Adams

OAK-RHIND, H.H. 'The Adams family: pipemakers', *Suffolk review* 5(5), 1977, 237-46. Includes pedigree, 17-19th c.

Adamson

See Oakes

Alderman

'Extracts from the register of Capel S.Mary, Suffolk', *East Anglian* **5**, 1893-4, 114-6. Relating to the Alderman, Bradstreet and Partridge families.
'Suffolk pedigrees', *M.G.H.* 5th series, **9**, 1935-7, 70-73. Alderman, 17-18th c., Aldrich of Rumburgh, 17-18th c., includes Aldrich wills.

Aldrich

'Suffolk pedigrees', *M.G.H.* 5th series, **9**, 1935-7, 101-2. Aldrich family, 18-19th c.
See also Alderman

Alexander

PEARSON, WILLIAM C. 'Extracts from parish registers: family of Alexander, Hemingston, Co.Suffolk', *East Anglian* N.S. **7**, 1897-8, 6-8.
'Suffolk pedigrees: Alexander of Framlingham', *M.G.H.* 5th series, **9**, 1935-7, 134-8. 17-19th c.
See also Wyncoll

Alington

HERVEY, ARTHUR. 'Horseheath and the Alingtons', *S.I.A.* **4**, 1863, 111-22. 14-18th c.

Allen

See Constable

Appleton

APPLETON, WILLIAM S., ed. *Family letters from the Bodleian Library, with notes.* Cambridge: C.U.P., 1902. Appleton family, 17th c., includes pedigree.

Applewhaite

'Suffolk pedigrees: Applewhaite of Huntingfield', *M.G.H.* 5th series, **9**, 1935-7, 177-8. 17-18th c.

Archer-Burton

See Constable

Bacon

PALMER, WILLIAM LINCOLN. 'Bacon family of Helmingham and Winston, Co.Suffolk, and of Dedham and Salem, Mass.', *New England Historical and Genealogical Register* **90**, 1936, 300-02. 15-17th c.
P[ARTRIDGE], C. 'Bacon of Friston', *E.A.M.* **1932**, 55. 16-17th c.
PEARSON, WILLIAM C., & PINK, W.D. 'The Bacons of Shrubland Hall, Co.Suffolk', *East Anglian* N.S. **4**, 1891-2, 33-5 and 49-54. See also 83-4. Parish register extracts and monumental inscriptions from Barham and Coddenham.
PEARSON, WILLIAM C. 'Extracts from parish registers', *East Anglian* N.S. **4**, 1891-2, 328-9. Relating to the Bacon family of Hemingstone, Barking, Rushmere St.Andrews, etc., 16-18th c.
PEARSON, WILLIAM C. 'Suffolk marriage licences, Ipswich Probate Registry. Bacon of Shrubland Hall', *East Anglian* N.S. **5**, 1893-4, 77-8. 16-17th c.
RYE, WALTER. *The false pedigree and arms of the family of Bacon of Suffolk, the ancestors of Sir Nicholas Bacon, of Francis Bacon (Lord Verulam) and of the present premier baronet, critically examined and exposed.* Norwich: Roberts & Co., 1919. 11-16th c.
TOWNSHEND, CHARLES HERVEY. 'The Bacons of Virginia and their English ancestry', *New England historical and genealogical register* **37**, 1883, 189-98. Originally of Suffolk, medieval– 17th c.
'Bacon and Buers', *M.G.H.* 3rd series, **4**, 1902, 160-67. Pedigrees, medieval-17th c.
See also Gosnold

Badeley

'Suffolk pedigrees: Badeley', *M.G.H.* 5th Series **9**, 1936, 190-91. 17-18th c.

Baden

See Powell

Baden-Powell

See Powell

Barnard

BARNARD, JOHN. 'The Barnard shipyards', *Suffolk review* N.S. **8**, 1987, 1-17. See also **10**, 1988, 38-41. Barnard family, 18th c.

Barnardiston

ALMACK, R. 'Kedington alias Ketton, and the Barnardiston family', *S.I.A.* **4**, 1863, 123-63. 12-18th c., includes wills, with lists of lords of manors and clergy.

Barnardiston *continued*

W., L.H.H. 'The Barnardiston family', *E.A.M.* **1933**, passim. 17-18th c.

Barrow

ROUND, J.H. 'An early citizen squire', *Ancestor 2*, 1902, 58-61. Barrow family of London and Barrow, 12-13th c.

Battelle

BATTELLE, LUCY CATHERINE. *A history of the Battelle family in England*. Columbus: Battelle Press, 1985. 13-20th c., of Suffolk, Derbyshire, Hampshire, Essex, etc. Includes pedigree.

Bayley

LEATHER, JOHN. 'The shipbuilding Bayleys', *Mariners Mirror* **51**(2), 1965, 131-45. 18-19th c.

Beadle

See Catelyn

Beaumont

GROWSE, F.S. 'Beaumont family', *East Anglian* **1**, 1858-63, 73-4. Includes pedigree, 16-17th c.

PEARSON, WILLIAM C. 'Beaumonts of Witnesham', *East Anglian* N.S. **4**, 1891-2, 127-8. Parish register extracts, Witnesham, Hemingstone, Barking and Barham.

'Pedigree: Beaumont of Hadleigh', *East Anglian* N.S. **1**, 1885-6, 130-31. 16-17th c.

See also Vere

Bedingfield

KENNEDY, ARTHUR J. CLARK. 'Bedingfield: from the parish registers of Darsham, Suffolk', *Genealogist* **2**, 1878, 29. Bedingfield family.

P[ARTRIDGE], C. 'Bedingfield of Bedingfield', *E.A.M.* **1933**, 64-5. Parish register extracts, 16-17th c.

Bence

WHAYMAN, HORACE W. ' Bence of Aldeburgh and Orford, Suffolk', *East Anglian* N.S. **6**, 1895-6, 332. 17th c. pedigree.

Berners

WARWICK, MARY ALICE SPENCER. *Some pictures from the past history of the Berners family.* Ipswich: W.E. Harrison, 1907.

Betham

BETHAM-EDWARDS, M. 'Some notes on the Betham family', *Eastern Counties Magazine* **1**, 1900-01, 190-05, and 312-17. Mainly 18-19th c.

Betts

DOUGHTY, KATHARINE FRANCES. *The Betts of Wortham in Suffolk, 1480-1905*. John Lane, The Bodley Head, 1912. Includes pedigree.

Bigg

See Ray

Bigod

TASBURGH, DOUGLAS. 'The Bigods and their castle of Bungay', *Eastern Counties Magazine* **2**,1901, 59-64. Medieval.

See also Felton

Bixby

THRELFALL, JOHN B. 'The English ancestry of Joseph Bixby of Ipswich and Boxford, Massachusetts', *New England historical and genealogical register* **141**, 1987, 228-43. 15-17th c., includes notes on Nunn.

Blennerhasset

MORIARTY, G. ANDREWS. 'Genealogical research in England: the East Anglian Blennerhassets', *New England historical and genealogical register* **98**(3), 1944, 271-9. Includes pedigree, 14-16th c., of Cumberland, Norfolk and Suffolk.

Blomfield

BLOMFIELD, REGINALD. 'A Suffolk family: being an account of the family of Blomfield in Suffolk. Chiswick Press: 1916. Includes pedigree, 12-19th c., list of wills, parish register extracts, etc.

PEARSON, WILLIAM C. 'Extracts from parish registers', *East Anglian* N.S. **4**, 1891-2, 136-8. Blomfield family; extracts from Barking, Hemingston and Henley.

PEARSON, WILLIAM C. 'Extracts from parish registers: Stonham Aspal', *East Anglian* N.S. **4**, 1891-2, 81-3 and 99-101. Blomfield family.

'Extracts from parish registers, Stonham Parva, Co.Suffolk', *East Anglian* N.S. **4**, 1891-2, 115-9. Blomfield family, 16-19th c., includes monumental inscriptions.

Boby

HUFFEY, G. 'Boby marriages', *S.Rt.* 4(3), 1978, 28. Parish register extracts, Boby family, 1673-1945.

Bohun

McCONELL, RICHARD B. *Ancestral peregrinations*. Houston: C.G. Fleetwood, 1979. Includes pedigrees, medieval-19th c.

Bokenham

See Bukenham

Booty

BOOTY, HAROLD. *The Bootys of Norfolk, Suffolk, Kent and Devonshire.* Privately issued, 1983. Includes pedigrees, 16-20th c.

Brackley

See Mannock

Bradstreet

See Alderman

Brewse

P[ARTRIDGE], C. 'Brewse of Little Wenham', *E.A.M.* **1934**, 52-3 and 54-5. Parish register extracts, 16-17th c.

Brewster

F., E. 'Brewster family', *E.A.M.* **1907**, 66, 68-9, 70-1, 72-3, 82-3 and 85. See also 87, 94 and 103; **1908**, 33, 46, 49, 62, 65-6 and 104-5; **1909**, 23. 15-17th c.

'Brewster: extracts from the Wrentham registers relating to the family of Brewster', *M.G.H.* N.S. **2**, 1877, 399-401. 17-18th c.

'Exemplification of arms and grant of crest to Humphrey Brewster of Rushmere, 1561', *M.G.H.* N.S. **2**, 1877, 325-6.

Bright

BRIGHT, J.B. *Brights of Suffolk, England represented in America by the descendants of Henry Bright, Jnr., who came to New England in 1630 and settled in Watertown, Massachusetts.* Boston, Mass.: John Wilson & Son, 1858. Includes pedigree, 16-18th c.

WHITMORE, W.H. 'Family of Bright, of Suffolk', *New England historical and genealogical register* **13**, 1859, 97-8.

Brownrigg

P[ARTRIDGE], C. 'Brownrigg of Willisham', *E.A.M.* **1934**, 18-19, 19-20, 21-22, 22-3, 24-6 and 33. Includes wills, parish register extracts, etc., 16-18th c.

Buckingham

RAIMONDO, HILARY. *Our company before: a history of the Buckingham family in East Anglia and New Zealand, 1682-1982.* Kensington Park, S.A.: Hilary Raimondo, 1987. Norfolk, Suffolk and New Zealand.

Buers

See Bacon

Bukenham

MAUDSLEY, HENRY. *Notes and extracts from numerous authorities respecting the family of Bukenham or Bokenham of Norfolk and Suffolk, from A.D.1066 to A.D.1883, and the places of that designation in the first named county.* Privately printed, 1884.

Bures

BURR, CHAUNCEY REA. 'Bures of Suffolk, England, and Burr of Massachusetts Bay Colony, New England. New York: Aldus Printers, 1926.

Burrough

CURTIS, HENRY, 'Portraits by Gainsborough of the allied family of Burrough of Sudbury', *Notes and queries* **175**, 1938, 128-30; **182**, 1942, 2-6 and 16-19. See also **175**, 1938, 152. 18th c., includes much genealogical information.

Burrows

R[EDSTONE], V.B. 'Burrows family', *E.A.M.* **1937**, passim. Extracts from Woodbridge and Ipswich parish registers and monumental inscriptions.

Burward

RATH-MERRILL, RUTH. 'A pedigree of the Burward or Burwood family of Dallinghoo, Woodbridge and Melton, Suffolk', *East Anglian* N.S. **6**, 1895-6, 220. 17-18th c.

Byles

CLEGG, MURIEL. 'Hill House and the Byles family in nineteenth century Ipswich', *Suffolk review* N.S. **2**, 1984, 1-4.

Cage

CARTHEW, GEO. A. 'Cage of Suffolk', *M.G.H.* N.S. **3**, 1880, 448-9. 17th c.

Call

ROMANES, CHARLES S. *The Calls of Norfolk and Suffolk: their Paston connections and descendants.* Edinburgh: T.& A.Constable, 1920. 14-20th c.

Calver

'Calver of Kenton and Thorndon', *E.A.M.* **1932**, 17-18. 16-17th c.

Canham

CULLUM, GERY MILNER GIBSON. 'Extracts from the register of Brent-Eleigh, Co.Suffolk, relating to the family of Canham', *M.G.H.* 2nd series **2**, 1888, 58. 17-18th c.

Capel

See Lofft

Caron
See Catlyn

Carver
'Carver', *M.G.H.* 5th series **8**, 1932-4, 139-42.
Pedigree, 18th c., with wills.

Castleton
OLORENSHAW, J.R. 'Extracts from parish registers:
Castleton family', *East Anglian* N.S. **5**, 1893-4,
323; see also N.S. **6**, 1895-6, 7.
'The family of Castleton of Stuston Hall', *East
Anglian* **3**, 1866-8, 249-50. Parish register
extracts, 17-18th c.

Catelyn
'Families of Catelyn and Beadle', *M.G.H.* N.S. **4**,
1884, 418-9. Extracts from family bible, 17th c.

Catlyn
W., E.L. 'Catlyn of Woolverston Hall, Suffolk:
families of Caron and Jenney', *East Anglian*
N.S. **9**, 1901-2, 46-8. 16-17th c.

Chapman
See Torlesse

Chaucer
REDSTONE, VINCENT B. 'The Chaucer-Malyn
family, Ipswich', *S.I.A.* **12**, 1906, 184-99.
Includes pedigree of Chaucer and Malyn;
medieval.

Chickering
CHAMBERLAIN, GEORGE WALTER. 'The English
ancestry of the Chickerings of New England',
*New England historical and genealogical
register* **69**, 1915, 226-9. Includes extracts from
Wrentham parish register, 17th c.

Church
PEARSON, WILLIAM C. 'Extracts from parish
registers', *East Anglian* N.S. **4**, 1891-2, 301-2.
Church, Martin and Lea families, of
Coddenham.
See also Southwells

Clare
ALTSCHULL, MICHAEL. *A baronial family in
medieval England: the Clares, 1217-1314*.
Baltimore: Johns Hopkins Press, 1965. Includes
pedigrees.
ROUND, J.H. 'The family of Clare', *Archaeological
Journal* **56**, 1899, 221-31. Medieval.
WARD, JENNIFER C. 'The estates of the Clare family,
1066-1317', *Bulletin of the Institute of
Historical Research* **37**, 1964, 114-17.
Summary of a thesis.
See also De Clare

Clark
See Rainbird

Clayton
YOUNG, E. 'Family of Clayton of Southolt,
Bedfield, etc.', *East Anglian* N.S. **10**, 1903-4,
204-7. 17-18th c.

Clopton
HOWARD, JOSEPH JACKSON & HART, WILLIAM HENRY,
eds. *The Cloptons of Suffolk, extracted from the
'Visitation of Suffolke'*. Lowestoft: Samuel
Tymms, 1865. Includes parish register extracts,
wills, etc., with pedigree, 12-17th c.

Coe
BARTLETT, J. GARDNER. *Robert Coe, Puritan, his
ancestors and descendants, 1340-1910, with
notes of the other Coe families*. Boston, Mass.:
the author, 1911. Includes pedigrees.
W., L.H.H. 'Coe of Mildenhall', *E.A.M.* **1932**, 31-2
and 33. Parish register extracts, 17-18th c.

Coggeshall
BEAUMONT, GEORGE FREDERICK. 'Coggeshall
family', *East Anglian* N.S. **1**, 1885-6, 221-3.
See also 263; N.S. **5**, 1893-4, 79, 142 and 203-5;
N.S. **7**, 1897-8, 9; N.S. **12**, 1907-8, 385; N.S. **13**,
1909-10, 176. 17-18th c.
W[AYMAN], H.W.B. 'Henry Coggeshall of Orford,
inventor and mathematician', *S.I.A.* **18**, 1924,
53-65. Includes pedigree, 17-18th c.

Colchester
PEARSON, W.C., 'Extracts from parish registers',
East Anglian N.S. **4**, 1891-2, 195-8. See also
223. Colchester and Goodwin families,
Barking, Stonham Parva, etc., parish registers.

Cole
COLE, JAMES EDWIN. *The genealogy of the family of
Cole, in the county of Devon, and those of its
branches which settled in Suffolk, Hampshire,
Surrey, Lincolnshire and Ireland*. John Russell
Smith, 1867. 13-19th c.

Collett
CHADD, MARGARET. *The Collett saga*. Norwich:
Elvery Dowers, 1988. Includes pedigrees,
16-20th c.

Colvile
COLVILE, SIR CHARLES, et al. *History of the Colvile
family*. Edinburgh: privately printed, 1896.
Suffolk, Yorkshire and Lincolnshire, 11-19th c.,
includes pedigrees.

Colville
See Deynes

Family Histories, Pedigrees, etc. *continued*

Constable

PARTRIDGE, C. 'Constable's paternal ancestry', *E.A.M.* **1934**, 70, 71-2, 74-5 & 77-8. See also **1935**, 8, 11, 41 and 48; **1936**, 79. 17-19th c.

John Constable's correspondence. S.R.S. **4, 6, 8, 10 & 12**, 1962-8. The first volume includes a brief family history, with pedigrees of Constable, Watts, Gubbins, Archer-Burton and Allen families. The 5th vol. includes a list of Constable's descendants.

Copinger

COPINGER, WALTER ARTHUR, ed. *History of the Copingers, or Coppingers, of the county of Cork, Ireland, and the counties of Suffolk and Kent, England.* New ed. Manchester: H. Sotheran, 1884. Includes pedigrees, 15-19th c.

Corbould

ROUND, J. HORACE. 'Corbould family', *Genealogist* N.S. **2**, 1885, 94-5. Includes pedigree, 17th c.

Cornwallis

MORIARTY, G. ANDREWS. 'The early generations of Cornwallis of Brome', *New England historical and genealogical register* **110**, 1956, 122-7. 14-16th c.

Corsellis

See Cullum

Cotman

See Hooker

Crane

APPLETON, WILLIAM S. *Memorials of the Cranes of Chilton, with a pedigree of the family, and the life of the last representative.* Cambridge, Mass.: John Wilson & Son, 1868. Includes pedigree, 13-17th c.

Craske

'Craske of Drinkstone', *E.A.M.* **1924**, passim. Parish register extracts, wills, etc.

Crickmer

See Sheppard

Crisp

CRISP, F.A. ed. *Collections relating to the family of Crispe.* 5 vols. F.A.Crispe, 1882-1913. v.1: Abstracts of wills and administration in the Prerogative Court of Canterbury, 1510-1760. v.2: Grants of arms, funeral certificates and pedigrees from the records of the College of Arms. v.3: Abstracts of wills and administrations in the courts of the Archdeacon of Suffolk, 1454-1800. v.4: Miscellanea. N.S. 1. Further and final extracts ... from the records of the College of Arms.

Crisp *continued*

P[ARTRIDGE], C. 'Crisp family', *E.A.M.* **1930**, 21-2. Of Chediston, 16-17th c.

Crowfoot

'Extracts from Sotterley register', *M.G.H.*, N.S. **4**, 1884, 40 and 50-51. Crowfoot family; includes extracts from Sotterley, Henstead, Uggeshall and Sotherton parish registers, 16-17th c.

Crowley

MARSHALL, G.W. 'Pedigree of the family of Crowley of Greenwich, Co.Kent, and of Barking, Co.Suffolk', *East Anglian* **3**, 1866-8, 95-8. 18th c.

Cullum

CULLUM, GERY MILNER GIBSON. 'Cullum', *M.G.H.* 2nd series **1-5**, 1886-94, passim. Includes innumerable extracts from registers, monumental inscriptions and wills.

CULLUM, GERY MILNER GIBSON. 'The family of Cullum', *M.G.H.* 4th Series **3**, 1910, 333-6. Includes monumental inscription and extracts from registers of Hawstead, 19th c.

CULLUM, GERY MILNER GIBSON. *Genealogical notes relating to the family of Cullum ...* Mitchell Hughes & Clarke, 1928. Includes pedigrees of Cullum, Levett, Hanson, Pake, Smith, Myddelton, Isaack, Jackson, Ray, Wittewronge, Gery, Le Heup and Corsellis, with many wills, parish register extracts, etc.

Cutler

'Grant of arms to Robert Cutler of Ipswich, by William Camden, Clarenceux, 1612', *M.G.H.* **1**, 1868, 228-9.

Cutting

See Gipps

Dade

Genealogical memoranda relating to the family of Dade of Suffolk. Mitchell & Hughes, 1888. Many extracts from miscellaneous original sources, 16-18th c.

'Dade notes', *M.G.H.* 2nd series, **1**, 1886, 199-204, 246-7, 268, 277-9; **2**, 1888, 11-12, 16, 49-51, 80 and 83-5.

Dameron

PEARSON, WILLIAM C. 'Extracts from parish registers ... family of Dameron', *East Anglian* N.S. **5**, 1893-4, 189-90.

Dandy

STEER, FRANCIS W. 'The Dandy pedigree', *S.I.A.* **27**, 1958, 133-53. Discussion of a pedigree compiled in the 16th c.

'Family of Dandy', *East Anglian* **2**, 1864-6, 164-6. Includes pedigree, 16-17th c.

Family Histories, Pedigrees, etc. *continued*

Danforth

BOOTH, JOHN. *The home of Nicholas Danforth in Framlingham, Suffolk, England, in 1635*. Framlingham: Framlingham Historical and National History Society, 1954. 16-17th c.

MAY, JOHN JOSEPH. *Danforth genealogy: Nicolas Danforth, of Framlingham, England, and Cambridge, N.E. (1589-1638) and William Danforth of Newbury, Mass. (1640-1721) and their descendants*. Boston, Mass.: C.H.Pope, 1902.

Darley

TOWEY, PETER. 'The Darleys of Suffolk', *S.Rt.* **13**(4), 1987, 93-4. 16-17th c.

Debenham

DEBENHAM, FRANK. *Seven centuries of Debenhams*. Glasgow: Robert Maclehose & Co., 1958.

SWEETING, WALTER DEBENHAM, ed. *A record of the family of Debenham of Suffolk*. St.Catherine Press, 1909. Includes pedigree, 18-19th c.

De Clare

RYE, WALTER. 'The De Clares in Suffolk (Earls of Gloucester) and the De Clares of Ormesby and Stokesby in Norfolk', *Genealogist* N.S. **37**, 1921, 169-73. 12-13th c.
See also Clare

De Gray

CRABBE, GEORGE. 'The De Grays of Little Cornard', *S.I.A.* **6**, 1888, 13-40. Includes pedigree of De Gray, 14-17th c., and of Frowyks, 15-16th c., with many lists of names extracted from rentals, court rolls, etc.
See also Gray

De La Pole

HARVEY, A.S., ed. *Homeland of the De La Poles: Kingston-upon-Hull and Wingfield in Suffolk*. Hull: privately printed, 1934.

ROUND, J.H. 'Note on the De La Pole pedigree', *Genealogist* N.S. **3**, 1886, 112.

RAVEN, JOHN JAMES. 'History of the De La Poles', *S.I.A.* **7**, 1891, 51-6. Medieval.

Denny

DENNY, C.C. *Genealogy of the Denny family in England and America, descendants of John Denny of Combs, Suffolk, England in 1439*. Leicester, Mass.: C.C.Denny, 1886. Includes pedigree, wills, deeds, etc.

DENNY, H.L.L. 'Pedigrees of some East Anglian Dennys', *Genealogist*, N.S. **38**, 1921, 15-28. Of Suffolk and Norfolk, 15-18th c.

Denny *continued*

DENNY, H.L.L. 'Some pedigrees of Denny, Le Denneys, etc.', *S.I.A.* **19**, 1927, 313-37. 13-19th c.

De Vere

See Spring, Stuffe and Vere

Devereaux

See Withipoll

Deynes

'Extracts from parish registers', *East Anglian* N.S. **4**, 1891-2, 380-2. Deynes and Colville families of Gosbeck, Barking and Hemingstone, etc.
See also Dove

Dove

PEARSON, WILLIAM C. 'Extracts from parish registers', *East Anglian* N.S. **4**, 1891-2, 284-5. For Dove family of Gosbeck, Barking, etc., 16-18th c.

'Extracts from parish registers', *East Anglian* N.S. **4**, 1891-2, 148-51. Families of Dove, Deynes, Hovell alias Smith and Killimarshe, from Coddenham, Barham, etc.

Dowsing

P., G.R. 'Birthplace of Dowsing the Iconoclast: the Dowsings of Laxfield', *East Anglian* **2**, 1864-6, 359-62. Gives many birth and death dates, 16-17th c.

'The family of William Dowsing', *E.A.M.* **1933**, 73-4, 17th c. Of Coddenham.

D'Oyly

See Thorrowgood

Drury

CAMPLING, ARTHUR. *The history of the family of Drury in the counties of Suffolk and Norfolk from the Conquest*. Mitchell, Hughes & Clarke, 1937. Includes pedigrees.

Eden

SPERLING, C.F.D. 'Ballingdon Hall and the Eden family', *Essex Archaeological Society Transactions,* N.S. **18**, 1928, 169-71. Of Ballingdon Hall, Essex, and Suffolk; includes pedigrees, 16-18th c.

Edgar

'The Edgar family of the Red House, Ipswich, and their interest in a faculty pew in St.Margaret's Church', *East Anglian* N.S. **10**, 1903-4, 118-20. Mainly 18th c.

Gray

HONAN, ROBERT F. *The Gray matter: the Gray family history, 16th to 20th century* ... Adelaide: Lutheran Publishing House, 1987. Of Berkshire, Hampshire, Oxfordshire, London and Middlesex, Suffolk and Australia; includes pedigrees.
See also De Gray

Greene

WILSON, R.G. *Greene King: a business and family history*. Bodley Head, 1983. Includes pedigrees of Greene, King and Maulkin families, 17-20th c.

Grigg

See Powell

Grimstone

'Extracts from the parish register of Rishangles, Co.Suffolk', *East Anglian* N.S. **8**, 1899-1900, 146. Grimstone family.

Gurteen

PAYNE, SARA. *The Gurteens of Haverhill: two hundred years of Suffolk textiles*. Cambridge: Woodhead-Faulkner, 1984. Includes pedigree, 18-20th c.

Guyver

P[ARTRIDGE], C. 'Guyver of Tilty, Essex and Milden, Suffolk', *E.A.M.* **1929**, 81. 17th c.

Hall

See Rainsford

Hammond

WILBY, ROBERT. 'Hammonds of Framlingham', *R. & B.* **6**(1), 1991, 5-7. 19-20th c.

Hanson

See Cullum

Harper

See Withipoll

Hart

See Rainsford

Harvey

PARTRIDGE, C. 'Harvey of Old Newton', *E.A.M.* **1915**, 2-3, 8-9, 10-11, 13-14, 15, 17, 21, 23, and 27-8. 17-18th c.

Harward

See Powell

Harwood

HARWOOD, ALFRED. *The Harwoods of Suffolk*. East Bergholt: [the author?], 1933. Includes pedigree, 16-20th c., also Studds family pedigree, 14-19th c.

Hasted

See Ray

Heigham

GREENING, SYLVIA. 'The Heighams of Barrow Hall', *Pagus* **7**, 1984, 8-12; **8**, 1984, 3-6. 16-18th c.

HEIGHAM, CHARLES WILLIAM. *Pedigree of the Heigham family*. Lowestoft: Samuel Tymms, 1876. Includes pedigrees, wills, parish register extracts, etc., 14-19th c.
See also Ray

Hempstead

BURGESS, RITA C. 'Hempsteads of Suffolk and Middlesex', *S.Rt.* **13**(4), 1987, 88-90; **14**(1), 1988, 16-17; **14**(2), 1988, 48. 19th c.

Henicames

F., E. 'Family of Henicames or Hingham, of Suffolk and Norfolk', *E.A.M.* **1907**, 27, 33, 40, 44-5 and 47-8. 17-18th c., includes wills and deeds.

Hervey

HERVEY, LORD ARTHUR. 'Ickworth and the family of Hervey', *S.I.A.* **2**, 1859, 291-429. Includes pedigrees, 9-18th c., with list of M.P.'s for Bury St.Edmunds, 17-19th c.

H[ERVEY], S.H.A. *Dictionary of Herveys of all classes, callings, counties and spellings from 1040 to 1500*. 5 vols. S.G.B. **20**. Ipswich: W.E. Harrison, 1924. v.1: Bedford to Middlesex. v.2: Norfolk. v.3: Suffolk. v.4: Northants to Yorks. v.5: Indexes.

H[ERVEY], S.H.A. *Hervey, first Bishop of Ely, and some others of the same name, 1050 to 1500, from Domesday, public records, and chronicles*. S.G.B. **19**. Ipswich: W.E. Harrison, 1923.

PONSONBY, D.A. *Call a dog Hervey*. Hutchinson, [1949]. Earls of Bristol, 17-18th c.

TIGHE, W.J. 'The Herveys: three generations of Tudor courtiers', *S.I.A.* **36**(1), 1985, 8-15. Includes pedigree, 15-17th c.

'Bookplate of John Hervey, esq.', *M.G.H.* 3rd series **5**, 1904, 296. 17-18th c. genealogical and heraldic notes.

Heveningham

P[ARTRIDGE], C. 'Heveningham of Heveningham', *E.A.M.* **1931**, 68-9. Parish register extracts.

Heynes

'Grant of arms by Robert Corke, Clarenceux, to Simon Heynes, of Mildenhall, Co.Suffolk, gentleman, 1575', *M.G.H.* **1**, 1868, 250-51.

Hingham

See Henicames

Holt

HOWARD, JOSEPH JACKSON, ed. *The Holts of Suffolk, extracted from 'the visitation of Suffolke'*. Lowestoft: Samuel Tymms, 1867. Pedigrees, 15-17th c., includes wills.

Hoo

TOWNSHEND, CHARLES HERVEY. 'Hesset (Suffolk, England) items', *New England historical and genealogical register* **38**, 1884, 342-3. Relating mainly to Hoo family; also including will of John Goodrich, 1632.

Hooker

ALLAN, MEA. *The Hookers of Kew, 1785-1911*. Michael Joseph, 1967. Also of Norfolk and Suffolk; includes pedigree, 17-20th c., with Vincent and Cotman pedigrees, 18-19th c.

Hopton

RICHMOND, COLIN. *John Hopton: a fifteenth century Suffolk gentleman*. Cambridge: C.U.P., 1981. Includes pedigrees of Hopton, 15-16th c., and Swillington, 14-15th c.

RUTTON, W.L. 'Pedigree of Hopton of Suffolk and Somerset', *M.G.H.* 3rd series, **3**, 1900, 9-12, 49-53 and 81-6. See also 3rd series, **4**, 1902, 151. 15-17th c.

Hovell

See Deynes

Howard

BRENAN, GERALD & STATHAM, EDWARD PHILLIPS. *The house of Howard*. Hutchinson, 1907. 13-20th c., includes various pedigrees.

CAUSTON, H. KENT STAPLE. *The Howard papers, with a biographical pedigree and criticism*. Henry Kent Causton & Son, [1862].

HOWARD, HENRY. *Indications of memorials, monuments, paintings and engravings of persons of the Howard family, and of their wives and children, and of those who have married ladies of the name, and of the representatives of some of its branches now extinct ...* Corby Castle: privately printed, 1834. Medieval-19th c., includes pedigrees.

RICHARDSON, ETHEL M.E. *The lion and the rose: (the great Howard story): Norfolk line, 957-1646, Suffolk line, 1603-1917*. 2 vols. Hutchinson, [1922].

ROBINSON, JOHN MARTIN. *The Dukes of Norfolk*. Oxford: Oxford University Press, 1983. Howard family; includes pedigrees, 14-20th c., with a select bibliography. Of Suffolk, Norfolk, Sussex and Derbyshire.

Howard *continued*

An analysis of the genealogical history of the family of Howard, with its connections ... H.K. Causton, 1812. Includes pedigrees, 11-19th c.

Hoxton

REID, L.W. 'The English ancestry of the Hoxtons of Maryland and Virginia', *Virginia Magazine of History and Biography* **60**(1), 1952, 115-68. 15-20th c., includes wills, etc.

Hull

'Pedigrees and heraldic notes from the collections of Gregory King, Lancaster Herald', *M.G.H.* 5th series, **10**, 1938, 93-4 and 104-7. Pedigrees of Hull, 17th c., and Fitch, 16-18th c.

Hunnings

FOSTER, W.E. *Some notes on the families of Hunnings of South Lincolnshire, London and Suffolk*. Exeter: William Pollard, 1912. Supplement to *Genealogist* N.S. **28-9**. Includes pedigrees, 13-19th c.

Isaack

CULLUM, GERY MILNER GIBSON. 'Isaack of Hitcham, Co.Suffolk and Jackson of Bury St.Edmunds in same county', *M.G.H.* 3rd series **3**, 1900, 56-9 and 76-80. Pedigree, 17-19th c., includes wills and parish register extracts.

'Pedigree of Isaack of Glemsford, Co.Suffolk', *M.G.H.* 3rd series, **3**, 1900, 54-5. 17th c.

See also Cullum

Jackaman

P[ARTRIDGE], C. 'Jackaman family', *E.A.M.* **1930**, 8. Of Mendlesham, 14-17th c.

Jackson

See Cullum

James

C., R.C. 'Family of James, of London, Essex, Kent, Suffolk, and Surrey', *East Anglian* **1**, 1858-63, 330-31. 16-19th c.

Jeaffreson

JEAFFRESON, M.T. *Pedigree of the Jeaffreson family, with notes and memoirs*. Privately printed, 1922. 16-19th c. Includes pedigrees.

Jennens

HARRISON, [W. & T.], & WILLIS, [G.], eds. *The great Jennens case: being an epitome of the history of the Jennens family*. Sheffield: Pawson & Brailsford, 1879. Includes pedigrees, 17-19th c., with many extracts from original documents.

Jenney

P[ARTRIDGE], C. 'Jenney family', *E.A.M.* **1933**, 69-70 and 88. Parish register extracts, 16-18th c. See also Catlyn

Jermy

VALDAR, STEWART. *A brief history of the Jermy family of Norfolk and Suffolk.* [New ed.]. London: the author, 1976. Includes pedigree, 13-20th c.

Jewell

See Game

Johnson

'Johnson of Aldborough', *East Anglian* N.S. **3**, 1889-90, 198. See also 214. Pedigree, 16-17th c.

Josselyn

JOSSELYN, J.H. *Genealogical memoranda relating to the family of Josselyn.* Ipswich: privately printed, 1903.

Katelyn

S., F.H. 'The Katelyn and Leman families', *East Anglian* N.S. **11**, 1905-6, 84-6. 17-18th c.

Keble

P[ARTRIDGE], C. 'Keble family', *E.A.M.* **1930**, 71-2 and 73. 17th c.

Kedington

See Kerrington

Kemball

PARTRIDGE, C.S. 'Kemball of Layham, Suffolk', *East Anglian* N.S. **4**, 1891-2, 276; N.S. **5**, 1893-4, 210-11; N.S. **6**, 1895-6, 366-7. Extracts from registers.

Kempe

HOWARD, JOSEPH JACKSON, ed. *The Kempes of Suffolk, extracted from 'the visitation of Suffolke'.* Lowestoft: Samuel Tymms, 1867.

Kerrington

L., W.M. 'Kerrington or Kedington family', *E.A.M.* **1932**, 56-7. Parish register extracts.

Killimarshe

See Deynes

King

KING, RUFUS. 'Extracts from the parish registers of Edwardstone, Suffolk, relating to the family of King', *M.G.H.* N.S. **4**, 1884, 68-9.
See also Greene

Kipling

See Powell

Kytson

HOWARD, JOSEPH JACKSON, ed. *The Kytsons and Gages of Hengrave, Suffolk, extracted from 'the visitation of Suffolke'.* Lowestoft: Samuel Tymms, 1867.

Ladbrook

Souvenir of a century: the story of W. Ladbrook & Son Ltd, 1848-1948. Bemrose & Sons, [1948]. Includes pedigree, 19-20th c.

Lane

CRAIG, ALGERNON TUDOR. 'Lane of Campsea Ash, Co.Suffolk', *M.G.H.* 5th Series **2**, 1916-17, 57-9. Pedigree, 16-18th c.

Last

W[AYMAN], H.W.B. 'Last of Orford, Co.Suffolk', *E.A.M.* **1907**, 76 and 78-9. See also 86. 19th c.

Launce

FELLA, THOMAS. *A memorable note wherein is conteyned the names in part of the cheefest kindred of Robert Launce, late of Mettfeild in the county of Suff., deceased, collected faithfully out of an old booke of his own handwriting ...* Privately printed, 1902. Facsimile reproduction of document copied in 1611.
'Launce family', *M.G.H.* N.S. **4**, 1884, 104-6. Notes from a 17th c. ms.

Lea

See Church

Le Denneys

See Denny

Lee

SUCKLING, F.H. 'Some notes on the Lee family of Lawshall in the county of Suffolk', *Genealogist* N.S. **23**, 1906, 137-43. See also p.271-2. 17-18th c.

Leeds

See Torlesse

Leeke

See Yaxley

Leeks

KIMBER, J. 'The Leeks family of Suffolk', *S.Rt.* **16**(4), 1991, 202-5. 17-20th c.

Le Heup

CULLUM, GERY MILNER GIBSON. 'Pedigree of the family of Le Heup, etc., wills, etc.', *M.G.H.* 4th series **2**, 1908, 198-201 and 236-40. 18th c., includes wills and extracts from parish registers of Hesset, Suffolk, and Spitalfields, London.

Le Heup *continued*

'Pedigree of the Huguenot family of Le Heup, together with those of Montolieu, Lowndes-Stone, etc., their descendants', *M.G.H.* 4th series **2**, 1908, 114-8 and 157-63. 18-19th c.

See also Cullum

Leman

See Katelyn

Lepingwell

LEPINGWELL, K. 'Lepingwell', *S.Rt.* **5**(1), 1979, 9-10. General discussion of the family's history, 13-20th c.

Levett

See Cullum

List

P[ARTRIDGE], C. 'List of Debenham and Cottenham', *E.A.M.* **1931**, 86-7. 17-18th c., List family.

Lofft

HAWES, HAROLD. 'Capel Lofft: some genealogical notes', *Suffolk review, 3*, 1966, 86-90. Includes pedigree of Maddocks, Capell and Lofft, 18-20th c.

Love

PEARSON, W.C. 'A list of kinsfolks ... of Richard Love ...', *East Anglian* N.S. **4**, 1891-2, 259-62.

Lucar

See Withipoll

Lucas

HOWARD, JOSEPH JACKSON, ed. *The Lucases of Suffolk, extracted from 'the visitation of Suffolke'*. Lowestoft: Samuel Tymms, 1867.

Macro

ALDRED, MARGARET G. 'The Macro family of Little Haugh', *Notes and queries, 200*, 1955, 188-91. 17-18th c.

Maddockes

HOLDEN, E. LOFFT. 'Entries relating to the Maddockes family', *Genealogist* **3**, 1879, 141-3. Of Suffolk and Surrey, 17-18th c. Includes will of Kinsman Singleman, 1769.

See also Lofft

Malyn

See Chaucer

Mannock

PARTRIDGE, C. 'Heraldic puzzle: Mannock and Brackley', *Notes and queries* **151**, 1826, 421. See also 466. 14-17th c.

Martin

G., W. 'The Martin family of Hadleigh', *E.A.M.* **1920**, 96, 98 and 100. Extracts from a family bible, 17-18th c.

See also Church

Maulkin

See Greene

Meadowe

PEARSON, WILLIAM C. 'Daniel Meadowe sometime of Chattisham Hall', *East Anglian* N.S. **5**, 1893-4, 49-51. Includes pedigree, 18th c.

W., H.A. 'Extracts from parish registers: Chattisham, Co.Suffolk: family of Meadowe', *East Anglian* N.S. **5**, 1893-4, 90-91.

Middleton

PEARSON, W.C. 'The Middletons of Crowfield Hall, afterward of Shrubland Hall, Co.Suffolk', *East Anglian* N.S. **4**, 1891-2, 77. Extracts from Coddenham and Barham parish registers.

Moise

See Moyse

Monson

'Monson', *M.G.H.* 3rd series **1**, 1896, 145. Extracts from Bacton parish register, 16-18th c.

Montchensi

FOWLER, G. HERBERT. 'Montchensi of Edwardstone and some kinsmen', *M.G.H.* 5th series **10**, 1938, 1-10. Includes pedigree, 12-14th c.

Moody

REED-LEWIS, WILLIAM, ed. *Some genealogical notes regarding the Moodys of Co.Suffolk, and America*. Bedford: F. Hockliffe, 1899. Includes pedigree, 17-18th c., with extracts from parish registers.

'Pedigree: Moody of Suffolk and America', *East Anglian* N.S. **2**, 1887-8, 38-9. 16-17th c.

Moore

BRIGHOUSE, URSULA. *Great Grandmamma used to say ...* Clyst St.Mary: Westprint, 198-? Moore of Kentwell, Suffolk; includes pedigree, 17-20th c.

Morgan

PEARSON, WILLIAM C. 'Extracts from parish registers: family of Morgan', *East Anglian* N.S. **7**, 1897-8, 99-101 and 235-8.

Moseley

HOLDEN, E.L. 'Moseley family: extracts from the registers of Owsden, Co.Suffolk', *Genealogist* **3**, 1879, 53-4. 17-18th c.

Moyse

GOLDING, C. 'Moyse or Moise family of Woodbridge, Co.Suffolk: extracts from fly-leaves in family bible', *M.G.H.* N.S. **2**, 1877, 127. 17-18th c.

Muriel

MURIEL, J.H.L. *A Fenland family: some notes on the history of a family surnamed Muriel.* Ipswich: East Anglian Magazine, [1968]. Extracts and notes from original documents, 13-19th c. Cambridgeshire, Isle of Ely, Suffolk, etc.

Myddleton

See Cullum

Naunton

STEER, FRANCIS W. 'The Naunton pedigree and family papers', *S.I.A.* **29**, 1964, 34-66. 11-18th c.

Nevill

NEVILL, EDMUND R. 'Nevills of Suffolk', *Genealogist* N.S. **31**, 1915, 141-53. 15-19th c.

Noble

P[ARTRIDGE], C. 'Noble of Livermere and Ampton', *E.A.M.* **1931**, 9 and 10. 16-18th c.

Notcutt

NOTCUTT, MICHAEL EDWARD. *The Notcutt family history, 1515-1989.* Chatham: Bachman & Turner, 1989. Somerset and Suffolk family, includes pedigrees, 16-20th c.

Nunn

W[AYMAN], H.W.B. 'Family of Nunn, of Orford', *E.A.M.* **1907**, 72. 18th c.

'Nunn of Stonham Earl, Co.Suffolk, now of Ardwick, Co.Lancaster, and Lawton, Co.Chester', *M.G.H.* 2nd series **2**, 1888, 89. 18-19th c.

See also Bixby

Oakes

FISKE, JANE, ed. *The Oakes diaries: business, politics and the family in Bury St.Edmunds. v.1: Introduction; James Oakes' diaries, 1778-1800.* S.R.S. **32**. Woodbridge: Boydell Press, 1990. Includes pedigrees of Oakes, Adamson and Ray families, 18-19th c.

See also Ray

Oxer

GOODING, A. 'Items from Suffolk parish registers', *S.Rt.* **2**(2), 1976, 24. Relating to 18th c. Oxer family.

Packard

PACKARD, J.J. *The Packards.* The author, 1987. Includes pedigree, 17-20th c.

Pake

See Cullum

Palgrave

PALGRAVE, DEREK A., & PALGRAVE-MOORE, PATRICK T.R. *History and lineage of the Palgraves.* Doncaster: Palgrave Society, 1978. Of Norfolk and Suffolk, 12-20th c. Includes many pedigrees and brief biographies.

PALMER, CHARLES JOHN & TUCKER, STEPHEN, eds. *Palgrave family memorials.* Norwich: Miller & Leavins, 1878. Of Barningham, Northwood, Thuxton, Pulham, Great Yarmouth and Coltishall; includes pedigree, 16-19th c., with extracts from original documents.

Partridge

M., W. 'Partridge of Great Welnetham, etc., Co.Suffolk', *East Anglian* N.S. **8**, 1899-1900, 190-1. Parish register extracts and list of probate records.

P[ARTRIDGE], C. 'Partridge family', *E.A.M.* **1935**, 59-60, 64-5 and 68-9. Parish register extracts, 16th c.

PARTRIDGE, CHARLES S. 'Partridge of Holton S.Mary, Suffolk', *East Anglian* N.S. **4**, 1891-2, 364-5. Parish register extracts.

PARTRIDGE, CHARLES S. 'Partridge of Shelley Hall, Co.Suffolk', *East Anglian* N.S. **7**, 1897-8, 12-13; **9**, 1901-2, 90-92, 142-5, 238-40 and 363-5; **10**, 1903-4, 58-60, 89-91, 138-41 and 299-301.

W., M. 'Some notes on Partridge of East Anglia before A.D.1500', *East Anglian* N.S. **6**, 1895-6, 313-4.

See also Alderman

Paske

GARDNER, C. 'The Paskes of Creeting St.Peter', *Suffolk review* **4**(2), 1973, 16-19.

Paston

See Call

Payne

HOWARD, JOSEPH JACKSON, ed. *The Paynes of Suffolk, extracted from 'the visitation of Suffolke'.* Lowestoft: Samuel Tymms, 1867.

Peche

ANDREWS, HERBERT C. 'Notes on some families and brasses of Great Thurlow and Little Bradley, Suffolk', *S.I.A.* **20**, 1930, 43-7. Includes pedigree showing connections of Peche, Gedding and Underhill, etc., 13-16th c.

Peyton

'Early history of the Peyton family', *Genealogical quarterly* **1**, 1932-3, 32-6, 121-3, 233-4 and 333-4. 13-17th c.

Philbrick

See Felbrigge

Playter

P[ARTRIDGE], C. 'Playters of Sotterley', *E.A.M.* **1931**, 75, 78 and 81-2. Parish register extracts, 16-18th c.

WADLEY, THOMAS P. 'Notes on the family of Playter or Playters of Co.Suffolk', *Genealogist* N.S. **1**, 1884, 45-9, 169-78 and 243-56. See also N.S. **3**, 1886, 117-8.

Poley

HERVEY, ALFRED. 'Boxted Hall: family of Poley', *S.I.A.* **3**, 1863, 358-74. 12-18th c.

HOWARD, JOSEPH JACKSON, ed. *The Poleys of Suffolk, extracted from 'the visitation of Suffolke'.* Lowestoft: Samuel Tymms, 1866.

'Badley parish register: Poley entries', *E.A.M.* **1925**, 17-18, 19, 21, 24, 25, 27, 32 and 33-34. 16-18th c.

Powell

POWELL, EDGAR. *Pedigree of the families of Powell and Baden-Powell; also of Sparke of Hawstead, Grigg of Suffolk, Harwood of Wiltshire and Kipling of Baldersdale.* William Clowes & Sons, 1926. 15-20th c.

POWELL, EDGAR. *Pedigree of the family of Powell, sometime resident at Mildenhall, Barton Mills and Hawstead in Co.Suffolk, and afterwards at Homerton and Clapton, Co.Middlesex and elsewhere, from Henry VII to Victoria, to which are added pedigrees of the families of Baden and Thistlethwaite of Co.Wilts.* E. Powell, 1891.

Preston

RYE, WALTER. 'A family legend: the emerald ring of the Preston family', *Ancestor* **2**,1902, 82-90. Includes 16-17th c. pedigree.

Pretye

'Family of Pretye', *Reliquary* **12**, 1871-2, 124. Undated pedigree from Harleian mss. 1560.

Pretyman

SWEETING, W.D. 'Pretyman family of Bacton, Suffolk', *East Anglian* N.S. **1**, 1885-6, 209-11. See also 246-7. Includes pedigree, 18th c.

Punchard

PUNCHARD, E.G. 'The family of Punchard', *East Anglian* N.S. **5**, 1893-4,, 104-7. Includes pedigree, 15-19th c.

Rainbird

DAVIES, S. 'Rainbird or Clark: search for an identity', *S.Rt.* **15**(3), 1989, 116-9. See also **16**(3), 1990, 168-9. 19th c.

Rainsford

BUCKLAND, EMILY A. *The Rainsford family, with sidelights on Shakespeare, Southampton, Hall and Hart, embracing 1000 years of the Rainsford family ...* Worcester: Phillips & Probert, 1832. Of Essex, Norfolk, Suffolk, Oxfordshire, Gloucestershire, Worcestershire, Warwickshire, Northamptonshire and various other counties; includes pedigrees.

Ransome

GRACE, D.R., & PHILLIPS, D.C. *Ransomes of Ipswich: a history of the firm and guide to its records.* Reading: Institute of Agricultural History, 1975. Includes pedigree of Ransome family, 18-20th c.

Rattle

RATTLE, THOMAS W. *The Rattle family.* Toronto: the author, 1968. Includes pedigrees, 17-20th c.

Ravett

'Ravett family: entries on fly-leaves of a bible ...', *M.G.H.* 2nd series **3**, 1890, 391-3. Bramfield; 19th c.

Rawlinson

See Ray

Ray

CULLUM, GERY MILNER GIBSON. *Pedigree of Ray of Denston, Wickhambrook and other places in Suffolk, together with Oakes of Nowton, Rawlinson of Stowlangtoft, Heigham of Hunston, Hasted, etc., all of the said county.* Mitchell & Hughes, 1903. 15-19th c.

CULLUM, GERY MILNER GIBSON. 'Ray of Denston, Wickhambrook and other places in Suffolk, together with Oakes of Nowton, Rawlinson of Stowlangtoft, Heigham of Hunston, Hasted and other families, all of the said county', *M.G.H.* 3rd series **5**, 1902-3, 219-27 and 246-8; 4th series **1**, 1905-6, 17-31 and 45-53. See also 5th series **7**, 1929-31, 15-16. Pedigree, 17-19th c.

Ray *continued*

MORIARTY, C.A. 'Ray—Gilbert—Bigg—Rowning', *New England historical and genealogical register* **104**, 1950, 107-14. Includes extracts from various sources, 16th c.
See also Cullum and Oakes

Reeve

GRAHAM, N.H. 'The Reeve family of Suffolk', *Notes and queries*, N.S. **1**, 1954, 508-11. Includes pedigree, 16-19th c.

Revett

See Rivett-Carnac

Reymes

RAIMES, ALWYN L. 'The family of Reymes of Wherstead in Suffolk, with some notes on the descendants of Roger de Rames of 1086', *S.I.A.* **23**, 1939, 89-115. Includes medieval pedigrees and deeds.

RAIMES, ALWYN L. 'Two Suffolk branches of the Reymes family', *S.I.A.* **27**, 1958, 25-33. Includes medieval pedigree.

Rhudde

DOW, LESLIE. 'The Rhudde family' in BECKETT, R.B., *John Constable's discourses.* S.R.S. **14**, 1970, 93-5. 17-19th c.

Richardson

RICHARDSON, E.A. 'Richardson ancestors', *S.Rt.* **15**(2), 1989, 82-5. 18-19th c.

Risby

'The Risby family', *E.A.M.* **1909**, 23, 28, 30-31, 37-8 and 43-4. 16-17th c.

Rivers

P[ARTRIDGE], C. 'Rivers of Chattisham', *E.A.M.* **1934**, 75-6. Includes parish register extracts.

Rivett-Carnac

RIVETT-CARNAC, J.H. *Notes on the family of Rivett-Carnac and its descent from Revett of Stowmarket and Brandeston Hall, Suffolk.* Rougemont, Switzerland: privately published, 1909. 13-20th c.

Rix

RIX, T. 'Earliest proven ancestors of Trevor William Rix, Alpheton, Suffolk', *S.Rt.* **5**(1), 1979, 6-8. 17-19th c.

Robinson

See Torlesse

Roe

PEARSON, WILLIAM C. 'Extracts from parish registers: family of Roe, Barking, Co.Suffolk', *East Anglian* N.S. **7**, 1897-8, 235-8.
See also Roo

Roo

ROE, F. GORDON. 'Roo of Debach, Suffolk', *Notes and queries,* 12th Series **11**, 1922, 226-7. 16th c.

ROE, F. GORDON. 'Roo (Roe) of Dallinghoo and Henley, Suffolk', *Notes and queries* 12th Series **11**, 1922, 366-7, 448-9 and 528-9. 16-18th c.

Rookwood

F., E. 'Coldham Hall and the Rookwoods', *E.A.M.* **1924**, passim. 15-18th c.

'Vetustissima prosapia Rookewodorum de Stanningefilde in comitatu Suffolciae', *Collectanea topographica et genealogica* **2**, 1835, 120-47. Rookwood family; includes pedigrees, 14-19th c.

Rope

ROPE, H.E.G. 'Cransford and the Rope family', *Suffolk review* **2**, 1962, 133-8. 19th c., also gives descent of Cransford from 14th c.

Rose

M., T.T. 'Family of Rose', *East Anglian* N.S. **5**, 1893-4, 255. 18th c.

Roser

DOW, LESLIE. 'The Roser family at Hacheston', *S.I.A.* **29**, 1964, 345-7. 17th c.

Rowning

See Ray

Rushbrook

P[ARTRIDGE], C. 'Rushbrook family', *E.A.M.* **1907**, 103-4. See also 113. Medieval.

Rust

B., H.K. 'The Rust family', *E.A.M.* **1922**, 38 and 40. Parish register extracts.

Sancroft

BOYCE, CHARLES. 'The family of William Sancroft, Archbishop of Canterbury', *S.I.A.* **20**, 1930, 117-24. Includes pedigrees, 12-18th c.

RAVEN, JOHN JAMES. 'The Sancrofts', *S.I.A.* **7**, 1891, 69-76. 16th c.

Scarlett

'Pedigrees of Scarlett', *M.G.H.* 2nd series **1**, 1886, 223-4. Suffolk and Essex, 17th c.

Scott

S., T.W. 'Scott genealogy: a fragment', *East Anglian* N.S. **7**, 1897-8, 124-5. Pedigree, 17-18th c.

Scott *continued*

'Lineage of Richard Scott, of Providence, U.S.A.', *East Anglian* N.S. **4**, 1869-70, 29-31. 17th c.

Scrivener

L., H.R. 'Scrivener family', *E.A.M.* **1928**, 81-2 and 83; **1929**, 2, 5, 6, 9 and 12. Medieval-18th c.

Seaman

'The Seaman family', *E.A.M.* **1908**, 41-2. Extracts from Thorndon parish register, 17-18th c.

Seckford

BRISCOE, DALY. *A Tudor worthy: Thomas Seckford of Woodbridge.* Ipswich: East Anglian Magazine, 1978. Includes pedigree, 14-17th c.

REDSTONE, VINCENT BURROUGH. 'The Seckfords of Seckford Hall', *S.I.A.* **9**, 1897, 359-69. Includes pedigree, 12-17th c.

TITCOMBE, J.C. *An illustrated Seckfordian history, (ancient and modern) A.D.1587-A.D.1900.* Woodbridge: George Booth, 1900. Seckford family and its charity; includes pedigree, with notes on inmates and trustees etc., of the charity. See also Stubbe

Shakespeare

See Rainsford

Sharpe

BULLEN, R.F. 'Sharpe family of Bury St.Edmunds', *East Anglian* N.S. **13**, 1909-10, 274-5 and 298-301. 16-18th c.

Sheldrake

P[ARTRIDGE], C.S. 'Genealogical mss., 1767-1821', *East Anglian* N.S. **5**, 1893-4, 35-7. Relating to Sheldrake of Wetheringsett.

Sheppard

J., E.C. 'A family bible, 1744', *E.A.M.* **1922**, 7, 10, 11 and 13. Sheppard, Crickmer and Burton families of Norfolk and Suffolk.

Sherman

SHERMAN, THOMAS T. 'The Shermans of Yaxley in Suffolk, England', *New England historical and genealogical register* **59**, 1905, 397-400. Extracts from registers of Yaxley, Stoke by Nayland, and Ipswich, Suffolk; and Diss and Roydon, Norfolk.

Singleman

See Maddockes

Skippon

'Skippon family', *M.G.H.* N.S. **1**, 1874, 37-40. See aslo 64-5. 17th c.

Smee

See Smy

Smith

CULLUM, GERY MILNER GIBSON. 'Smith of Cavendish, Bacton and Thrandeston', *M.G.H.* 3rd series **1**, 1896, 177-84. Pedigree, 15-18th c., with extracts from Thrandeston parish register.

MUSKETT, J.H. 'A churchly family: the Smiths of Stratford', *East Anglian* N.S. **3**, 1889-90, 201-3. See also 220, 277-8 and 390. 15-17th c., Stratford St.Mary.

'Smith of Thrandeston', *East Anglian* N.S. **4**, 1891-2, 15, 31 and 360-2. See also 380.

'Thomas Smith of Bacton, 1620', *M.G.H.* 2nd series **5**, 1894, 1-2. Funeral certificate.

'Smith: parish register of Thrandeston, Co.Suffolk', *M.G.H.* 3rd series **1**, 1896, 185. 17-18th c.

See also Cullum and Deynes

Smy

P[ARTRIDGE], C. 'Smy family', *E.A.M.* **1935**, 78-9. Includes parish register extracts and will of Edward Smee, 1639-40.

Smythies

'Pedigree of the Smythies family', *M.G.H.* 4th series **4**, 1911, 170-82, 193-200, 276-86, 306-9 and 354-63. Somerset, Essex and Suffolk; 16-20th c.

Soame

'Soame of Suffolk and London', *East Anglian* N.S. **3**, 1889-90, 210-11. Pedigree, 17th c.

Southampton

See Rainsford

Southwell

PEARSON, WILLIAM C. 'Extracts from parish registers', *East Anglian* N.S. **4**, 1891-2, 314-7. Relating to Southwells, Church and Gosnold families of Barham, Hemingstone, etc.

Sparke

See Powell

Sparrow

GLYDE, J. 'Pedigree: Sparrow of Ipswich', *East Anglian* N.S. **1**, 1885-6, 190-1. See also 150.

PEARSON, WILLIAM C. 'Extracts from parish registers ... family of Sparrow', *East Anglian* N.S. **5**, 1893-4, 46-7.

Spring

HARPER, A. 'The Spring and De Vere families of Lavenham', *S.Rt.* **4**(4), 1978, 61-2. 15-18th c.

McCLENAGHAN, B. *The Springs of Lavenham and the Suffolk cloth trade in the XV and XVI centuries*. Ipswich: W.E. Harrison, 1924. Includes pedigree, 15-16th c.

Steyning

See Stubbe

Stiff

PHILLIMORE, WILLIAM P.W. *Memorials of the family of Stiff, of Norton and Rougham, in the county of Suffolk*. Stroud: White, 1885.

PHILLIMORE, WILLIAM P.W. 'Stiff or Steff of Suffolk', *M.G.H.* 2nd Series **4**, 1892, 224. 16-18th c.

Stubbe

DOW, LESLIE. 'Two sixteenth century marriage settlements', *S.I.A.* **26**, 1955, 144-7. Covers the marriages of John Stubbe and Anne De Vere, 1577, and Charles Seckford and Mary Steyning, 1575. Includes pedigree showing relationships.

Stubbin

PARTRIDGE, C.S. 'Stubbin of Raydon and Higham: extracts from the register of the parish of Holton St.Mary, Suffolk', *East Anglian* N.S. **4**, 1891-2, 245; N.S. **5**, 1893-4, 69-70.

Studds

See Harwood

Style

PEARSON, WILLIAM C. 'Extracts from parish registers ... family of Style', *East Anglian* N.S. **5**, 1893-4, 274-7.

Sulyard

DIMOCK, ARTHUR. 'Haughley Park and the Sulyards', *S.I.A.* **12**, 1906, 88-96. 15-19th c.

MURRAY, C.R.S., et al. 'Pedigree of the family of Sulyard of Wetherden and Haughley, Co.Suffolk and of Flemings, Co.Essex', *Genealogist* **4**, 1880, 226-34. 15-18th c.

'Sulyard of Wetherden', *E.A.M.* **1931**, 2-3 and 5. Extracts from the parish register, 16-19th c.

Swillington

See Hopton

Talmage

PEARSON, WILLIAM C. 'Extracts from parish registers ... the family of Talmage', *East Anglian* N.S. **5**, 1893-4, 140-42.

Talmage *continued*

PEARSON, WILLIAM C. 'The Talmages of Coddenham, Co.Suffolk', *East Anglian* N.S. **4**, 1891-2, 73-5. Parish register extracts.

Tasburgh

EVANS, NESTA. 'The Tasburghs of South Elmham: the rise and fall of a Suffolk gentry family', *S.I.A.* **34**, 1981, 269-80. Includes pedigree, 15-18th c.

Tastard

P[ARTRIDGE], C. 'Tastard family', *E.A.M.* **1929**, 87, 1930, 1-2 and 3. 14-19th c.

Taylor

ARMITAGE, DORIS MARY. *Taylors of Ongar: portrait of an English family of the eighteenth and nineteenth centuries, drawn from family records*. Cambridge: W. Heffer & Sons, 1939. Includes 18th c. pedigree. Also of Lavenham, Suffolk.

TAYLOR, ISAAC, ed. *The family pen: memorials, biographical and literary of the Taylor family of Ongar*. 2 vols. Jackson, Walford and Hodder, 1867. 18-19th c., also of Lavenham, Suffolk.

Theobald

PEARSON, WILLIAM C. 'Pedigree of Theobald of Barking Hall', *East Anglian* N.S. **4**, 1891-2, 158-9. 17-18th c.

Thistlethwaite

See Powell

Thorne

PEARSON, WILLIAM C. 'Extracts from parish registers ... family of Thorne', *East Anglian* N.S. **5**, 1893-4, 346-7.

'Thorne of Hemingstone', *E.A.M.* **1931**, 71, 72 and 73-4. Parish register extracts, 16-18th c.

See also Withipoll

Thorrowgood

P[ARTRIDGE], C. 'Thorrowgood and D'Oyly families', *E.A.M.* **1934**, 69-70. Parish register extracts, 17-18th c.

Tilney

BRISTOW, CYRIL. *Tilney families*. Tonbridge: the author, 1988. 12-20th c., includes many extracts from original documents.

Timperley

CORDER, J. SHEWELL. 'Hintlesham Hall', *Journal of the British Archaeological Association* N.S. **34**, 1928, 87-95. Timperley family, 15-16th c.

P[ARTRIDGE], C. 'Timperley of Hintlesham', *E.A.M.* **1931**, 50, 52, 53-4 and 58. See also 70 and 73. 18-19th c.

Timperley *continued*

RYAN, SIR GERALD H., & REDSTONE, LILIAN J. *Timperley of Hintlesham: a study of a Suffolk family*. Methuen & Co., 1931. 15-18th c., includes list of incumbents of Hintlesham church.

Tollemache

BOOTH, J. 'Tollemache of Helmingham', *E.A.M.* **1933**, 42 and 43-4. 16th c.

P[ARTRIDGE], C. 'Tollemache family', *E.A.M.* **1932**, passim. 13-18th c.

ROUNDELL, MRS. CHARLES. 'The Tollemaches of Bentley; the Tollemaches of Helmingham', *S.I.A.* **12**, 1906, 97-112. Mainly 16-17th c.

TOLLEMACHE, E.D.H. *The Tollemaches of Helmingham and Ham*. Ipswich: W.S. Cowell, 1949. 12-20th c. Includes pedigrees.

Torlesse

TORLESS, FRANCES H. *Bygone days*. Harrison & Sons, 1914. History of Torlesse, Robinson and Wakefield families, 18-19th c., includes pedigrees of Chapman, Fennell and Leeds as well as aforementioned.

Tradescant

ALLAN, MEA. *The Tradescants: their plants, gardens and museum, 1570-1662*. Michael Joseph, 1964. Includes pedigree, 16-17th c.

Turnour

'Turnour of Hauerell', *M.G.H.* 3rd series **4**, 1902, 184-6. Haverhill, Suffolk, and Essex, etc., undated pedigree.

Tyrrell

BROWN, O.F. *The Tyrrells of England*. Chichester: Phillimore, 1982. Of various counties, including Essex and Suffolk; pedigrees, 11-18th c.

P[ARTRIDGE], C. 'Tyrrell of Gipping', *E.A.M.* **1931**, 63. Parish register extracts, 17-18th c.

SEWELL, W.H. 'Sir James Tyrrell's Chapel at Gipping, Suffolk', *Archaeological journal* **28**, 1871, 23-33. Includes pedigree, 15-16th c.

Umfreville

See Wyncoll

Vere

PEARSON, WILLIAM C. 'Extracts from the register of Henley, Co. Suffolk', *East Anglian* N.S. **4**, 1891-2, 20-23. Primarily Vere and Beaumont families, 16-18th c.

See also Spring and Stubbe

Vincent

See Hooker

Wakefield

See Torlesse

Waldegrave

PROBERT, W.H.C. 'Waldegraves of Bures', *Essex review* **41**, 1932, 86-7. Bures St.Mary is a Suffolk parish, although it borders on Essex.

See also Wyncoll

Walpole

WALPOLE, J.A. 'Walpole notes from Yoxford registers', *E.A.M.* **1921**, 74.

Ward

MUSKETT, J.J. 'Pedigree of Ward of Suffolk and America', *New England historical and genealogical register* **41**, 1887, 282-4. 16-17th c.

Watts

See Constable

Webb

WATERS, R. E. CHESTER. 'Webb alias Wood', *M.G.H.* N.S. **1**, 1874, 14-15. Pedigree 17-18th c.

Wentworth

RUTTON, WILLIAM LOFTIE. *Three branches of the family of Wentworth*. The author, 1891. Of Suffolk, Essex and Oxfordshire. 15-19th c., includes pedigrees.

RUTTON, WILLIAM LOFTIE. 'Wentworth of Nettlestead', *East Anglian* N.S. **2**, 1887-8, passim. Includes pedigree, 15-19th c.

Wenyeve

BETHAM, CHARLES JEPSON. 'Brettenham and the Wenyeve family', *S.I.A.* **9**, 1897, 131-43. 15-17th c., includes monumental inscriptions.

Wightman

I'ANSON, BRYAN. *Records of the Wightman (Whiteman or Weightman) family*. Privately printed, 1917. Of Suffolk, Leicestershire and London. Includes wills, extracts from parish registers, etc., with pedigrees, medieval-20th c.

Wilkin

P[ARTRIDGE], C. 'Wilkin of Cornard Parva', *E.A.M.* **1936**, 56. 16-17th c., of Little Cornard.

Wingfield

DEWING, E.M. 'Pedigree of Wingfield', *S.I.A.* **7**, 1891, 57-68. 14-19th c.

PEARSON, WILLIAM C. 'Extracts from parish registers ... family of Wingfield', *East Anglian* N.S. **5**, 1893-4, 61-2.

POWERSCOURT, MERVYN EDWARD, VISCOUNT. *Muniments of the ancient Saxon family of Wingfield*. Mitchell & Hughes, 1894. Includes pedigrees, 14-19th c.

Wingfield *continued*

WINGFIELD, JOHN M., ed. *Some records of the Wingfield family.* John Murray, 1925. 15-20th c., includes pedigrees.

Winthrop

MASSACHUSETTS HISTORICAL SOCIETY. *Winthrop papers.* 4 vols. Boston, Mass.: the Society, 1929-47. Family papers, 1498-1649.

MUSKETT, J.J. *Evidences of the Winthrops of Groton, Co.Suffolk, England ...* Boston, Mass.: R.C. Winthrop, 1894-6. 15-17th c.

WINTHROP, ROBERT C. *Short account of the Winthrop family.* Cambridge: John Wilson & Son, 1887. 15-19th c.

Withipoll

DUNLOP, J.RENTON. *Pedigree of the Withipoll family of Somersetshire, Shropshire, Essex and Suffolk.* Mitchell, Hughes & Clarke, 1925. Reprinted from *M.G.H.* 5th series **5**, 1925, 378-86. 15-17th c.

SMITH, G.C. MOORE. *The family of Withypoll, with special reference to their manor of Christchurch, Ipswich, and some notes on the allied families of Thorne, Harper, Lucar, and Devereaux.* Walthamstow Antiquarian Society official publications, **34**. Letchworth: the Society, 1936. 15-18th c., includes pedigree.

Pedigree of Wythipol of Ipswich. East Anglian N.S. **10**, 1903-4, 302-4. 16-17th c.

Wittewronge

See Cullum

Wollaston

WATERS, ROBERT EDMOND CHESTER. *Genealogical memoirs of the elder and extinct line of the Wollastons of Shenton and Finborough, their ancestors and connections ...* Robson & Sons, 1877. Includes pedigrees, 14-17th c.

Wolsey

CASLEY, HENRY C. 'The position in life of Wolsey's family', *East Anglian* N.S. **2**, 1887-8, 21-3, 33-6, 57-8 and 74-5. 15-16th c.

REDSTONE, VINCENT B. 'Wulcy of Suffolk', *S.I.A.* **16**, 1918, 71-89. Medieval ancestors of Cardinal Wolsey.

Wolton

WOLTON, ERIC D. *A Suffolk family.* [ ]: privately printed, 1978. Wolton family, 17-20th c.

Wood

See Webb

Woodward

P[ARTRIDGE], C. 'Woodward family', *E.A.M.* **1932**, 5-6 and 7-8. In Hoxne and Hartismere hundreds.

P[ARTRIDGE], C. 'Woodward of E.Suffolk', *E.A.M.* **1929**, passim. Parish register extracts, wills, etc., 16-18th c.

Wren

GANDY, WALLACE. 'The Wren family of Suffolk, &c., showing Sir Christopher Wren's association with East Anglia', *S.I.A.* **18**, 1924, 52(f). Folded pedigree, 16-17th c.

Wulcy

See Wolsey

Wyncoll

SIER, L.C. 'The Wyncoll family', *Essex Archaeological Society transactions*, N.S. **11**, 1911, 236-45; N.S. **12**, 1913, 1-13, 101-8. Of Suffolk and Essex; includes pedigrees, 16-19th c.

WYNCOLL, CHARLES EDWARD. *The Wyncolls of Suffolk and Essex.* Colchester: [ ], 1911. Includes pedigrees, 16-19th c., of Wyncoll and related families, i.e. Gawdy, Waldegrave, Umfreville and Alexander.

Wythe

WYETH, MARION SIMS. *Nicholas and George Wythe: an account of a search for their English antecedents.* Palm Beach: privately printed, 1958. Includes pedigree, 17th c., extracts from parish registers, etc.

Yaxley

FARRER, EDMUND. 'Yaxley Hall: its owners and occupiers', *S.I.A.* **16**, 1918, 1-28 and 135-66. Yaxley family, 15-18th c., and Leeke family, 18-20th c. Includes Yaxley pedigree.

Young

THOMPSON, T.W. 'Youngs, Gibsons and their associates: an inquiry into the origin of certain East Anglian and metropolitan gypsy families', *Gypsy Lore Society journal* **24**, 1945, 44-56; **25**, 1946, 39-45. 18-20th c., Norfolk, Suffolk and Essex.

8. PARISH REGISTERS AND OTHER RECORDS OF BIRTHS, MARRIAGES AND DEATHS

Registers of births, marriages and deaths are normally one of the first sources to be consulted by the genealogist. For Suffolk, manuscript parish registers are listed in:

PALGRAVE-MOORE, PATRICK T.R. *National index of parish registers, vol.7: East Anglia: Cambridge, Norfolk and Suffolk.* Society of Genealogists, 1983.

Bishops transcripts from the Sudbury Archdeaconry are listed in:

REDSTONE, V.B. 'Records of the Sudbury archdeaconry, pt.1', *S.I.A.* **11**, 1902, 252-266.

Many extracts from bishops' transcripts of missing parish registers from West Suffolk are printed in:

BULLEN, R. FREEMAN. 'Some missing Suffolk parish registers', *E.A.M.* **1923**, passim.

The historical uses of bishops' transcripts are discussed in:

GRACE, FRANK. 'The bishops' transcripts for the Archdeaconry of Suffolk and their uses for the study of population', *Suffolk review* N.S. **1**, 1983, 8-14.

Various lists and calendars of marriage licences are available:

R[EDSTONE], V.B. 'Suffolk marriage licences, 1476-1515', *E.A.M.* **1936**, 39, 41 and 42. List of those in the Norwich Diocesan Registry.

[CRISP, F.A., ed.] *Marriage licences from the official note books of the Archdeaconry of Suffolk deposited at the Ipswich Probate Court, 1613-1674.* F.A. Crisp, 1903.

[CRISP, F.A., ed.] *Marriage licence bonds in the Suffolk Archdeaconry registry at Ipswich, 1663-1750.* F.A. Crisp, 1900.

'Marriage licence bonds', *E.A.M.* **1937**, 70. From Crisp's manuscript transcripts, 1753-1815.

BANNERMAN, W. BRUCE & BANNERMAN, G.G. BRUCE, eds. *Allegations for marriage licences in the Archdeaconry of Sudbury, in the county of Suffolk during the years 1684 to [1839].* 4 vols. Publications of the Harleian Society, **69-72**, 1918-21.

WHAYMAN, HORACE. 'Orford marriage licences, from the official note books of the Archdeaconry of Suffolk, deposited at the Ipswich Probate Court, 1613-1674', *East Anglian* N.S. **10**, 1903-4, 312-13.

Many birth, marriage and death notices, together with other miscellaneous information, e.g. bankrupts, are given in:

SAVOR, J. 'Extracts from the *Cambridge Chronicle and Journal,* 1810-1812', *S.Rt.* **9**(2), 1983, 31-2; **9**(3), 1983, 65; **10**(1), 1984, 17-18; **10**(2), 1984, 30; **10**(3), 1984, 62; **10**(4), 1984, 92-3.

Migration is the bane of the genealogist! Where did they come from is the question we all ask. Many 'stray' entries of Suffolk births, marriages and deaths have been published, especially in *E.A.M.* and *S.Rt.* The following list is a brief selection from extracts in these journals, and is arranged by county:

Essex

OSBORNE, D. 'Suffolk strays into Halstead, Essex', *S.Rt.* **5**(1), 1979, 5. Covers 1620-1753.

H., A.D. 'Marriages of Suffolk', *E.A.M.* **1933**, 3. At Witham, Essex.

Middlesex

BULLEN, R. FREEMAN. 'East Anglian marriages in Stepney registers', *E.A.M.* **1911**, 76, 78-9, 81-2, 83, 85-6, 89-90, 91, 98, 100-101, 103, 106, 108-9, 112, 117-8, 120-21, 123-4, 126-7 and 129-30; **1912**, 2-3, 5, 7-8, 10-11 and 13. Strays from Norfolk, Suffolk, Essex and Cambridgeshire, 1581-1719.

Lincolnshire

COLE, A. 'Suffolk strays from Lincolnshire', *S.Rt.* **16**(3), 1990, 144-5.

Norfolk

FARROW, C.W. 'The first parish register of St.Michael at Plea, Norwich, A.D.1538-1695, transcribed by Thomas R. Tallack, 1892', *S.Rt.* **3**(1), 1977, 52-3. Suffolk entries.

Northumberland

REDFERN, MR. 'Strays: burials, Newcastle upon Tyne', *S.Rt.* **16**(3), 1990, 145. 17th c. Suffolk strays.

Many individual parish registers have been published and are listed below. Also listed here are a variety of brief notes and extracts relating to particular parishes, together with a few non-Anglican registers. A word of warning: just because a register is in print does not mean that it is an accurate transcript. Some parish register editors did a good job; others were woeful! If you identify an entry in a printed register, check the original if you can.

Akenham

PEARSON, W.C. 'Extracts from the registers of Akenham, Co.Suffolk', *East Anglian* N.S. **9**, 1901-2, 43-6; reprinted in N.S. **11**, 1905-6, 51-4.

Aldeburgh

WINN, ARTHUR T. 'Commonwealth marriages and burials in the Aldeburgh register book', *Notes and queries* 12th Series **10**, 1922, 80-83, 104-6, 124-6 and 142-5. See also 175 and **11**, 1922, 295-6.

Ashby

YOUNG, E. & HALSEY, G., eds. 'Marriages at Ashby, 1553 to 1837', in BLAGG, THOMAS M., ed. *S.P.R.M.* **4**, *P.P.R.S.* **235**. Phillimore, 1931, 81-4.

Bardwell

WARREN, F.E., ed. *The registers of Bardwell, Co.Suffolk, 1538 to 1650*. Mitchell & Hughes, 1893. Reprinted from *M.G.H.* 2nd Series **5**, 1894, passim.

Barrow

W., L.H.H. 'Barrow registers', *E.A.M.* **1931**, 69-70 and 70-71. Brief note.

Boyton

W. 'Extracts from parish registers, no.34: Boyton, Suffolk', *East Anglian* 4, 1869-70, 217-20. 16-19th c.

Bradfield St.Clare

HASLEWOOD, FRANCIS. 'Parish register of Bradfield St.Clare, 1541 to 1595', *S.I.A.* **9**, 1897, 311-29. Transcript, with list of rectors, 1578-1873.

Bramfield

HILL, THOMAS S., ed. *Regestrie booke off Bramefeilde, off all christnyngs, weddyngs and buryings ... 1539-96 and 1693-1889*. Mitchell & Hughes, 1894. Reprinted from *M.G.H.* 2nd Series **3-4**, 1890-2, passim.

Bredfield

'Quakers buried at Bredfield, 1743-1778', *E.A.M.* **1942**, 28-9. List.

Brundish

[CRISP, F.A., ed.] *The parish registers of Brundish, Suffolk*. Privately printed, 1885. Covers 1562-1785.

Bury St.Edmunds

H[ERVEY], S.H.A., ed. *Bury St.Edmunds. St.James parish registers*. 3 vols. S.G.B. **17**. Bury St.Edmunds: Paul & Mathew, 1915-16. Baptisms, 1558-1800; marriages, 1562-1800; burials, 1562-1800.

POWELL, EDGAR. 'Extracts from parish registers, St.Marys, Bury St.Edmunds', *East Anglian* N.S. **4**, 1891-2, 110-11. 16th c.

Bury St.Edmunds *continued*

'Burials of pre-Reformation clergy at St.Mary's Church, Bury St.Edmunds, 1538-1574', *East Anglian* N.S. **12**, 1907-8, 65-6.

Buxhall

COPINGER, W.A. *History of the parish of Buxhall in the county of Suffolk ...* H.Sotheran & Co., 1902. Includes full transcript of parish register, 1558-1700, extracts from wills, 16th c. court rolls, etc.

Capel St.Mary

JOHNSON, A. CECIL, ed. 'Marriages at Capel St.Mary, 1538 to 1837', in PHILLIMORE, W.P.W., & BLAGG, THOMAS M., eds. *S.P.R.M.* **1**, *P.P.R.S.* **120**. Phillimore, 1910, 99-119.

P[ARTRIDGE], C. 'Capel S.Marys parish registers', *E.A.M.* **1934**, 59-60 and 62. Extracts relating to gentry, etc.

Carlton

[CRISP, F.A., ed.] *The parish registers of Carlton, Suffolk*. Privately printed, 1886. 1538-1886.

Chevington

BRIGG, WILLIAM, ed. *The parish registers of Chevington, co.Suffolk, 1559 to 1812*. Leeds: privately printed, 1915.

Chillesford

[CRISP, F.A., ed.] *Parish registers of Chillesford, Suffolk*. Privately printed, 1886. Covers 1740-1876.

Clare

ARMSTEAD, JOHN B. 'Clare parish registers', *East Anglian* 1, 1858-63, 42-3. Notes on the register.

Claydon

PEARSON, WILLIAM C. 'Extracts from the parish registers of Claydon, Co.Suffolk', *East Anglian* N.S. **11**, 1905-6, 100-3. Miscellaneous families.

Combs

LOWE, C.E., ed. 'Marriages at Combs, 1568 to 1837', in PHILLIMORE, W.P.W. & BLAGG, THOMAS M., eds. *S.P.R.M.* **1**. *P.P.R.S.* **120**. Phillimore, 1910, 121-56.

Culford

BRIGG, WILLIAM, ed. *The parish registers of Culford, co.Suffolk. Baptisms, marriages, burials, 1560-1778*. Leeds: privately printed, 1909.

Culpho

[CRISP, F.A., ed.] *The parish registers of Culpho, Suffolk*. Privately printed, 1886. Covers 1721-1882.

Dallinghoo
'Quakers buried at Dallinghoo', *E.A.M.* **1942**, 30-31.

Denham
CULLUM, SIR THOMAS GERY. 'Extracts from the registers of Denham, in the Hundred of Risbridge, Suffolk', *East Anglian* N.S. **4**, 1891-2, 230-33.

H[ERVEY], S.H.A., ed. *Denham parish registers, 1539-1850, with historical notes and notices.* S.G.B. **8**. Bury St.Edmunds: Paul & Mathew, 1904. Includes monumental inscriptions, wills, inquisitions post mortem, tax lists, pedigrees, etc., etc.

Depden
'Extracts from the register of Depden in the county of Suffolk', *East Anglian* **4**, 1891-2, 209-12. 16-18th c.

Drinkstone
CRESWELL, G.G. BAKER. 'Drinkstone parish registers', *East Anglian* N.S. **5**, 1893-4, 327-31, 366-7 and 375-8. Covers 1579-88.

Dunwich
YOUNG, EVELYN, ed. 'Marriages at Dunwich St.Peter, 1549 to 1658', in BLAGG, THOMAS M., ed. *S.P.R.M.* **4**. *P.P.R.S.* **235**. Phillimore, 1931, 97-114.

Ellough
[CRISP, F.A., ed.] *The parish registers of Ellough, Suffolk.* [ ]: privately printed, 1886.

Exning
FOSTER, J.E. 'Marriages at Exning, 1558 to 1812', in PHILLIMORE, W.P.W., & BLAGG, THOMAS M., eds. *S.P.R.M.* **1**. *P.P.R.S.* **120**. Phillimore, 1910, 29-62.

Fakenham Magna
P[ARTRIDGE], C. 'Fakenham Magna's registers', *E.A.M.* **1932**, 18-19. Extracts, 1609-1735.

Felixstowe
Transcript of baptisms, Old Felixstowe, 1796-1813. Felixstowe: Felixstowe F.H.S., c.1988.
Transcript of burials, Old Felixstowe, 1764-1812. Felixstowe: Felixstowe F.H.S., c.1987.
See also Walton

Freckenham
'Extracts from the parish registers of Freckenham, Suffolk', *East Anglian* N.S. **12**, 1907-8, 299. 17th c.

Fressingfield
RAVEN, A.J., ed. 'Marriages at Fressingfield, 1554 to 1837', in BLAGG, THOMAS M., ed. *S.P.R.M.* **4**. *P.P.R.S.* **235**. Phillimore, 1931.
RAVEN, J.J. 'Parish register entries in the Commonwealth period', *East Anglian* N.S. **9**, 1901-2, 84. For Fressingfield, 1658.

Frostenden
[CRISP, F.A., ed.] *The parish registers of Frostenden, Suffolk.* Privately printed, 1887. Covers 1538-1791.

Glemsford
W., L.H.H. 'Glemsford register', *E.A.M.* **1932**, 58-9 and 60. Brief description with list of curates and rectors.

Great Wenham
KEMBALL, R.W.J., ed. 'Marriages at Great Wenham, 1670 to 1837', in PHILLIMORE, W.P.W., & BLAGG, THOMAS M., eds. *S.P.R.M.* **1**. *P.P.R.S.* **120**. Phillimore, 1910, 157-63.

Great Whelnetham
H[ERVEY], S.H.A., ed. *Great Whelnetham parish registers, 1561 to 1850; Little Whelnetham parish registers, 1557 to 1850, with historical and biographical notes, illustrations, map and pedigrees.* S.G.B. **15**. Bury St.Edmunds: Paul & Mathew, 1910. Also includes a wide range of other sources, e.g. tax lists, wills, deeds, list of rectors, pedigrees, etc.

Grundisburgh
TAYLOR, MISS, ed. 'Marriages at Grundisburgh, 1539 to 1837', in BLAGG, THOMAS M., ed. *S.P.R.M.*, **4**. *P.P.R.S.*, **235**. Phillimore, 1931, 115-37.

Haverhill
ASHTON, W.D., 'Digging for roots', *Haverhill Historian* **6**, 1980, 8-11. Notes on registers of Haverhill Independent Church.

Henley
PEARSON, WILLIAM C. 'Surnames in parish registers, Henley: Suffolk', *East Anglian* N.S. **4**, 1891-2, 56-60. Lists, 1558-1889.

Henstead
'Extracts from parish registers, no.32: Henstead', *East Anglian* **4**, 1869-70, 107-8. 16th c.

Hepworth
METHOLD, THOMAS TINDAL. 'Early registers of Hepworth, Co.Suffolk', *East Anglian*, N.S. **5**, 1893-4, 23-4. Entries for 1565-9, plus a few from missing register for 1572-1684.

Holbrook

'Holbrook baptisms ...', *S.Rt.* **15**(4), 1989, 176. 37 entries from pre-1837 registers of Colchester Wesleyan Methodist Circuit and Ipswich Wesleyan Methodist Circuit.

Hollesley

BANNERMAN, W. BRUCE, ed. *The parish registers of Hollesley, co.Suffolk.* Parish Register Society publications, **82**. [1920] Covers 1596-1813.

Holton St.Mary

'Holton S.Mary's parish registers', *E.A.M.* **1934**, 68-9. Extracts, 16-19th c.

Hopton All Saints

P[ARTRIDGE], C. 'Dissenters children', *E.A.M.* **1931**, 57. List from Hopton All Saints register, 1698-1737.

Horham

P[ARTRIDGE], C. 'Horham's parish registers', *E.A.M.* **1935**, 20 and 22. Transcript of a few scraps, 1593-1627.

Horringer

H[ERVEY], S.H.A., ed. *Horringer parish registers: baptisms, marriages and burials, with appendixes and biographical notes, 1558 to 1850.* S.G.B. **4**. Woodbridge: George Booth, 1900. Appendices include monumental inscriptions, tax lists, clergy lists, etc.

Hoxne

RAVEN, ALEC J., ed. 'Marriages at Hoxne, 1548 to 1837', in RAVEN, ALEC J., ed. *S.P.R.M.* **3**. *P.P.R.S.* **223**. Phillimore, 1916, 1-52.

Ickworth

H[ERVEY], S.H.A. *Ickworth parish registers: baptisms, marriages and burials, 1566 to 1890.* S.G.B. **3**. Wells: Ernest Jackson, 1894. Includes monumental inscriptions, list of rectors, etc.

Ilketshall St.Margaret

EASTON, J.G. 'Notes on the earliest parish register of Ilketshall St.Margaret, Co.Suffolk', *East Anglian* N.S. **4**, 1891-2, 161-7. Notes with some extracts.

Ingham

BRIGG, WILLIAM, ed. *The parish register of Ingham, Co.Suffolk. Baptisms 1538 to 1804. Marriages, 1539 to 1787. Burials, 1538 to 1811.* Leeds: privately printed, 1909.

Ipswich

BURNHAM, R.E. 'Ipswich records', *R. & B.* **2**(2), 1987, 8. List of parish registers for Ipswich at Suffolk Record Office.

GRIMSEY, B.P. *Longevity in Ipswich: list of persons who have died in the borough of Ipswich between 1 Jan 1868 and 1 Jan 1889 ... 85 years and upwards.* Ipswich: S. and S.J. King, 1890. Gives ages, addresses and status/occupation.

L., H.R., ed. 'An Ipswich undertakers register', *E.A.M.* **1937**, passim; **1938**, 1 and 2-3. Lists 372 funerals, 1788-1831.

St.Margaret

'Notes on the early register books of St.Margaret's, Ipswich', *East Anglian* N.S. **10**, 1903-4, 147-51, 173-9, 190-3 and 201-4. Includes some extracts, 16-18th c.

St.Nicholas

COOKSON, EDWARD, ed. *The registers of St.Nicholas, Ipswich, Co.Suffolk: baptisms, 1539-1709; burials, 1551-1710; marriages, 1539-1710.* Parish Register Society, **7**. 1897.

St.Peter

[CRISP, F.A., ed.] *The parish registers of St.Peter's, Ipswich, 1662-1700.* F.A. Crisp, 1897.

St.Stephen

'Extracts from the register books of St.Stephen's, Ipswich', *East Anglian* N.S. **2**, 1887-8, 290-92. 17th c.

Ixworth Thorpe

COPINGER-HILL, H. 'Ixworth Thorpe', *E.A.M.* **1928**, 34. Transcript of odd pages of parish register for 1719.

Kelsale

[CRISP, F.A., ed.] *The parish registers of Kelsale, Suffolk.* Privately printed, 1887. Covers 1538-1812.

Knodishall

WINN, ARTHUR T., ed. *The register of the parish church of Knodishall, co.Suffolk, 1566-1705.* Bemrose & Sons, 1909.

Lavenham

'Lavenham parish register', *E.A.M.* **1936**, 39-40, 43, 44, 47-8 and 49. Brief description including burials of clergy, etc.

Laxfield

P., G.R. 'Extracts from parish registers, no.18: Laxfield, Suffolk', *East Anglian* **2**, 1866, 256-8. 17th c.

Letheringham

RUSHEN, PERCY C., ed. *Transcripts of the parish registers of Letheringham in the county of Suffolk, A.D.1588-1758 and 1812, and of all the sepulchral inscriptions and arms now and formerly within its church and churchyard, with notes on some of the persons named ... and an account of the said parish, its rectory, church, dissolved priory, etc.* Privately produced, 1901.

Little Saxham

H[ERVEY], S.H.A., ed. *Little Saxham parish registers: baptisms, marriages and burials, with appendices, biographies, etc., 1559 to 1850.* S.G.B. **5**. Woodbridge: George Booth, 1901. Appendices include inscriptions, tax lists, wills, inquisitions post mortem, clergy lists, etc.

Little Wenham

JOHNSON, A.C., ed. 'Marriages at Little Wenham, 1567-1812', in PHILLIMORE, W.P.W. & BLAGG, THOMAS M., eds. *S.P.R.M.*, **1**. *P.P.R.S.* **120**. Phillimore, 1910, 63-69.

Little Whelnetham

See Great Whelnetham

Long Melford

W., L.H.H. 'The Hospital of the Holy Trinity, Long Melford', *E.A.M.* **1934**, 6-7, 9, 14 and 23. Burial entries for the almshouse, 16-19th c.

Lowestoft

STEEL, J.P. & LONGE, F.D., eds. *Parish registers of Lowestoft in the county of Suffolk.* Lowestoft: Flood & Son, 1899. Covers 1561-1720.

[CRISP, F.A., ed.] *The parish registers of Lowestoft, Suffolk: Marriages, 1650-1750. Baptisms and burials, 1724-1750.* F.A. Crisp, 1901.

CRISP, F.A., ed. *Parish registers of Lowestoft, Suffolk: Marriages, 1752-1812. Baptisms and burials, 1751-1812.* F.A. Crisp, 1904.

LEES, HUGH D.W. 'Seafaring entries from the burial register, Lowestoft, Suffolk', *S.Rt.* **2**(3), 1976, 30-32. Covers 1815-66.

BARDWELL, KATHERINE. 'Dissenters', *S.Rt.* **10**(1), 1984, 9-10. Baptisms of dissenters children at St.Margarets, Lowestoft, 1709-11.

Martlesham

DOUGHTY, E.G., ed. 'Marriages at Martlesham, 1633 to 1837', in PHILLIMORE, W.P.W. & BLAGG, THOMAS M., eds. *S.P.R.M.* **1**. *P.P.R.S.* **120**. Phillimore, 1910, 71-98.

Mellis

CREED, HENRY. 'Extracts from the register of Mellis', *Proceedings of the Bury and West Suffolk Institute of Archaeology* **1**, 1853, 286-96. 1569-1787; includes only 'persons of note'.

Mendham

RAVEN, ALEC J., ed. 'Marriages at Mendham, 1678 to 1837', in his *S.P.R.M.* **3**. *P.P.R.S.* **233**. Phillimore, 1916, 75-103.

Metfield

BLAGG, T.M. & STUART, E.J., eds. 'Marriages at Metfield, 1559 to 1837', in RAVEN, ALEC J., ed. *S.P.R.M.* **3**. *P.P.R.S.* **233**. Phillimore, 1916, 105-30.

Mickfield

PERRY, CLEMENT RAYMOND, ed. 'Marriages at Mickfield, 1558 to 1837', in BLAGG, THOMAS M., ed. *S.P.R.M.* **4**. *P.P.R.S.* **235**. Phillimore, 1931, 139-52.

Mildenhall

W., L.H.H. 'Mildenhall register', *E.A.M.* **1932**, 64-5. Brief description with list of curates.

Monk Soham

MORLEY, CLAUDE, ed. *The registers of the parish of Monks' Soham, in the county of Suffolk.* Monks Soham: privately printed, 1920. Covers 1712-1919.

North Cove

X. 'Extracts from parish registers: North Cove, Suffolk', *East Anglian* **2**, 1864-6, 317. 18th c.

Otley

'Register book of births for Otley Baptist Chapel in the county of Suffolk, founded c.1800, PRO Ref RG4/1856', *S.Rt.* **8**(2), 1982, 27-8. Index of surnames in the register.

Pakenham

[CRISP, F.A., ed.] *The parish registers of Pakenham, Suffolk.* Privately printed, 1888. Covers 1566-1766.

Palgrave

MANNING, C.R. 'Register of Palgrave, Co.Suffolk', *East Anglian* N.S. **3**, 1889-90, 270-71. Selected entries, 1698-1705.

Pettaugh

PEARSON, WILLIAM C. 'Extracts from the registers of Pettaugh, Co.Suffolk', *East Anglian* N.S. **8**, 1899-1900, 358-60; **11**, 1905-6, 138-9. Relating to leading parishioners.

Poslingford

P[ARTRIDGE], C. 'Suffolk marriages at Heybridge, Essex', *E.A.M.* **1933**, 86. See also **1934**, 4. The entries are actually from the parish register of Poslingford, Suffolk, and were mistakenly attributed to Heybridge by Partridge.

Rattlesden

OLORENSHAW, J.R., ed. *Notes on the history of the church and parish of Rattlesden, in the county of Suffolk, together with copy of the parish registers from 1558 to 1758, and index of the marriages.* [Rattlesden]: the editor, 1900. Includes list of clergy and parish officers, wills, overseers accounts, etc., as well as the parish registers.

Risby

YOUNG, EVELYN, ed. 'Marriages at Risby, 1674 to 1837', in BLAGG, THOMAS M., ed. *S.P.R.M.* **4**. *P.P.R.S.* **235**. Phillimore, 1931, 85-95.

Rougham

W., L.H.H. 'Rougham registers', *E.A.M.* **1931**, 46, 47-8, 49 and 51. Brief description.

Rushbrooke

H[ERVEY], S.H.A., ed. *Rushbrooke parish registers, 1567 to 1850, with Jermyn and Davers annals.* S.G.B. **6**. Woodbridge: George Booth, 1903. Includes monumental inscriptions, lay subsidies, wills, and histories of the families of Jermyn, 1180-1703, Davers, 17-18th c., and Rushbrooke, 15-19th c.

Shotley

H[ERVEY], S.H.A., ed. *Shotley parish registers, 1571 to 1850, with all tombstone inscriptions in church and churchyard.* S.G.B. **16**(1). Bury St.Edmunds: Paul & Mathew, 1911. Includes rentals of 1380 and 1594, various pedigrees, and clergy list.

Somerleyton

YOUNG, EVELYN, ed. 'Marriages at Somerleyton, 1558 to 1837', in BLAGG, THOMAS M., ed. *S.P.R.M.* **4**. *P.P.R.S.* **235**. Phillimore, 1931, 63-79.

Stanton St.John

W., L.H.H. 'Stanton St.John parish registers', *E.A.M.* **1932**, 53-4. General description, with list of churchwardens.

Stoke Ash

RAVEN, J.J. 'Marriages of "foreigners" at Stoke Ash', *East Anglian* N.S. **9**, 1901-2, 102-5. 1687-1743 parish register extracts.

Stoke by Nayland

JARRETT, BEDE, ed. 'Catholic registers of Rev. James Dominic Darbyshire, O.P., at Standish and Borwich Hall, Warton, Lancashire, 1728; Gifford Hall, Stoke-by-Nayland, Suffolk, 1728, and Ugbrooke Park, Chudleigh, Devon, 1736-55', *Publications of the Catholic Record Society*, **25**, 1925, 247-52.

Stonham Aspall

PEARSON, WILLIAM C. 'The earliest register of Stonham Aspal, Co.Suffolk', *East Anglian* N.S. **7**, 1897-81, 75-7 and 93-5.

Stuston

'Extracts from parish registers, no.24: Stuston, Suffolk', *East Anglian* **3**, 1868, 60-61 and 89-90.

Stanningfield

The parish registers of Stanningfield, Suffolk. 4 vols. [Stanningfield]: [The Rector and Churchwardens?], 1897-8. Covers 1561-1812.

Sudbury

BRABROOK, K. 'Extracts from the records of persons buried in Friars Street Old Meeting Yard, Sudbury, Suffolk', *S.Rt.* **9**(2), 1983, 26. 1707-1822.

Syleham

RAVEN, ALEC J., ed. 'Marriages at Syleham, 1538 to 1837', in his *S.P.R.M.* **3**. *P.P.R.S.* **233**. Phillimore, 1916, 53-73.

Tannington

[CRISP, F.A., ed.] *The parish registers of Tannington, Suffolk.* F.A. Crisp, 1884. Covers 1539-1714.

Thorington

HILL, THOMAS S., ed. *The registers of the parish of Thorington in the county of Suffolk; with notes on the different Acts of Parliament referring to them, and notices of the Bence family, with pedigree, and other families whose names appear therein.* Mitchell & Hughes, 1884. Includes monumental inscriptions, and pedigree of Bence, 16-20th c.

Thorndon

C[RISP], F.A., ed. *Registers of Thorndon, Co.Suffolk.* [Privately printed], 1921. Covers 1538-1711.

Thrandeston

FRENCH, THOMAS LEE, ed. 'Marriages at Thrandeston, 1559 to 1812', in PHILLIMORE, W.P.W. & BLAGG, THOMAS M., eds. *S.P.R.M.* **1**. *P.P.R.S.* **120**. Phillimore, 1910, 1-27.

Thrandeston *continued*

'Marriages at Thrandeston, 1813 to 1837', in BLAGG, THOMAS M., ed. *S.P.R.M.* **4**. *P.P.R.S.* **235**. Phillimore, 1931, 153-6.

Timworth

BRIGG, WILLIAM, ed. *The parish register of Timworth, co.Suffolk: Baptisms, 1565-1716; Marriages, 1558-1715; Burials, 1572-1715*. Leeds: privately printed, 1909.

Tuddenham St.Martin

PEARSON, WILLIAM C. 'Extracts from the register of Tuddenham St.Martin, Co.Suffolk', *East Anglian* N.S. **11**, 1905-6, 164-8. Includes monumental inscriptions.

Tunstall

WAYMAN, H.W.B. 'Extracts from the parish registers of Tunstall, Co.Suffolk', *East Anglian* N.S. **13**, 1909-10, 36.

Walsham le Willows

W., L.H.H. 'Walsham-Le-Willows registers', *E.A.M.* **1935**, 91; **1936**, 3, 7 and 14-15. Brief description with list of churchwardens.

Walton

W., S.D. 'Burial grounds in Walton and Felixstowe', *E.A.M.* **1934**, 13 and 14. See also 17. List of cemeteries.

Westerfield

PEARSON, W.C. 'Memoranda in the oldest register of the parish of Westerfield, Co.Suffolk', *East Anglian* N.S. **4**, 1891-2, 289-9. Amongst other things, includes list of children being taught in 1687-88.

West Stow

H[ERVEY], S.H.A., *West Stow parish registers, 1558 to 1850; Wordwell parish registers, 1580 to 1850, with sundry notes*. S.G.B. **7**. Woodbridge: George Booth, 1903. Includes monumental inscriptions, tax lists, wills, clergy lists, notes on families, etc.

Westleton

W. 'Westleton, Co.Suffolk', *East Anglian* **3**, 1869, 304-7, 311-4 and 340-46; **4**, 1870, 1-2, 16 and 17.

Weybread

RAVEN, CANON, ed. 'Marriages at Weybread, 1687 to 1837', in BLAGG, THOMAS M., ed. *S.P.R.M.* **4**. *P.P.R.S.* **235**. Phillimore, 1931, 45-62.

Withersdale

RAVEN-HART, CANON, ed. 'Marriages at Withersdale, 1660 to 1837', in RAVEN, ALEC J., ed. *S.P.R.M.* **3**. *P.P.R.S.* **233**. Phillimore, 1916, 131-43.

Withersfield

W., L.H.H. 'Withersfield parish registers', *E.A.M.* **1933**, 45 and 48. Brief description, with list of churchwardens, etc.

Witnesham

M., S.M.W. 'Witnesham marriages', *E.A.M.* **1952**, 29-30, 31-2, 34, 36 and 38; **1953**, 2 and 26. Marriages of Witnesham inhabitants in other parishes, 17-19th c.

PEARSON, WILLIAM C. 'Memoranda in the parish registers of Witnesham', *East Anglian* N.S. **5**, 1893-4, 372-3. Gives names, but not births, marriages or deaths.

Woodbridge

'Marriages at Woodbridge, 1545 to 1837', in PHILLIMORE, W.P.W., BLAGG, THOMAS M. & TAYLOR, R. FETZER, eds. *S.P.R.M.* **2**. *P.P.R.S.* **167**. Phillimore, 1912, 1-166.

Wordwell

See West Stow

Yaxley

S., W.H. 'Extracts from parish registers, no.17: St.Marys, Yaxley, Suffolk', *East Anglian* **2**, 1866, 245-7.

9. MONUMENTAL INSCRIPTIONS

A. *GENERAL*

Monumental inscriptions are an important source of genealogical information, especially for the last two or three centuries. Their transcription has formed an important part of the work of the Suffolk Family History Society. This work remains unpublished; however, many Suffolk inscriptions are in print. The most important works are:

PARTRIDGE, CHARLES, ed. *Suffolk churchyard inscriptions copied from the Darby transcription (made about 1825-34)*. 3 vols. [ ]: Suffolk Institute of Archaeology and Natural History, 1913-23. Reprinted from *S.I.A.* **15, 17** and **18**. Contents: Pt.1. Hundreds of Babergh, Blackbourn, Blything and Bosmere-and-Claydon. Pt.2. Hundreds of Carlford, Colneis, Cosford, Hartismere, Hoxne, Lackford and Loes. Pt. 3. Hundreds of Mutford-Lothingland, Plomesgate, Risbridge, Samford, Stow, Thedwestry and Thingoe (part of).

MACCULLOCH, DIARMAID. 'Henry Chitting's Suffolk collections', *S.I.A.* **34**, 1980, 103-28. Mainly monumental inscriptions, copied in the 17th c.

Y., D.A. ' Summary catalogue of sepulchral memorials and remains of ancient art existing in parish churches', *Topographer and Genealogist* **1**, 1846, 161-75, 280-93, 474-91 and 538-56; **2**, 1853, 153-68, 234-46, 289-304, 385-97 and 494-505.

'Index to monumental inscriptions in Suffolk churchyards', *East Anglian* N.S. **7-10**, 1897-1904, passim.

A series of brief notes in the *East Anglian* on 'Suffolk church notes' was primarily devoted to monumental inscriptions:

BIRCH, H.W., 'Some Suffolk church notes', *East Anglian* N.S.

Barham	**6**, 1895-6, 177-82
Barking	**6**, 1895-6, 292-8
Baylham	**6**, 1895-6, 369-72
Belstead	**7**, 1897-8, 266-8
Bentley	**7**, 1897-8, 220-1
Bramford	**12**, 1907-8, 364-7; **13**, 1909-10, 8-9
Brantham	**8**, 1899-1900, 143
Burgh	**13**, 1909-10, 313-4
Burstall	**13**, 1909-10, 67-8
Capel St.Mary	**8**, 1899-1900, 247-8
Chelmondiston	**8**, 1899-1900, 42-4
Claydon	**13**, 1909-10, 171-3
Coddenham	**6**, 1895-6, 33-7
Copdock	**7**, 1897-8, 273-4
Crowfield	**5**, 1893-4, 340-1

General continued

East Bergholt	**12**, 1907-8, 309-11, 332-8 and 342-5
Elmsett	**7**, 1897-8, 167-71
Erwarton	**8**, 1899-1900, 104-8
Flowton	**7**, 1897-8, 106-7
Freston	**8**, 1899-1900, 68-70
Gosbeck	**5**, 1893-4, 313-4
Great Bealings	**13**, 1909-10, 261-4
Great Belstead	**7**, 1897-8, 273-4
Great Blakenham	**6**, 1895-6, 102-4
Great Wenham	**8**, 1899-1900, 196
Grundisburgh	**13**, 1909-10, 210-12 and 244-6
Harkstead	**8**, 1899-1900, 115-8
Hasketon	**13**, 1909-10, 295-7
Hemingstone	**5**, 1893-4, 353-6
Henley	**6**, 1895-6, 10-13
Hintlesham	**13**, 1909-10, 82-6
Holbrook	**8**, 1899-1900, 115-8
Holton St.Mary	**12**, 1907-8, 197-8
Ipswich, St.Clements	**9**, 1901-2, 39-41, 53-5 and 68-70
St.Helens	**9**, 1901-2, 127-31
St.Lawrence	**9**, 1901-2, 149-52 and 185-7
St.Margaret	**9**, 1901-2, 187-8, 202-5, 213-6 and 231-4
St.Mary at Elms	**9**, 1901-2, 253-4 and 265-9
St.Mary at the Quay	**9**, 1901-2, 291-2, 305-8 and 314-6
St.Mary at the Tower	**10**, 1903-4, 7-10, 29-31 and 38-42
St.Mary Stoke	**9**, 1901-2, 336-9
St.Matthew	**9**, 1901-2, 360-3 and 379-82
St.Nicholas	**10**, 1903-4, 52-6 and 71-3; **12**, 1907-8, 115-9
St.Stephen	**12**, 1907-8, 129-34
Kirton	**13**, 1909-10, 349-50
Little Bealings	**8**, 1899-1900, 219-22
Little Wenham	**13**, 1909-10, 279-80
Martlesham	**13**, 1909-10, 356-9
Needham Market	**6**, 1895-6, 309-11
Nettlestead	**6**, 1895-6, 153-7
Newbourn	**13**, 1909-10, 349-50
Raydon	**12**, 1907-8, 231-3
Shotley	**8**, 1899-1900, 22-3
Somersham	**6**, 1895-6, 153-7
Sproughton	**13**, 1909-10, 136-41
Stratford St.Mary	**12**, 1907-8, 145-9
Stutton	**13**, 1909-10, 181-3 and 205-8
Tattingstone	**8**, 1899-1900, 157-60
Tuddenham St.Martin	**6**, 1895-6, 356-8
Washbrook	**7**, 1897-8, 269-70
Wherstead	**13**, 1909-10, 147-9
Whitton-cum-Thurlestone	**6**, 1895-6, 213-5
Woolverstone	**8**, 1899-1900, 51-3

For inscriptions from the Hundred of Samford, see:

'Churchyard inscriptions from parishes in the hundred of Samford and county of Suffolk', *Register of English Monumental Inscriptions* **1**, 1911, 83-152.

Lists of transcripts, both printed and manuscript, are provided by:

O[SWALD]-H[ICKS], T.W. 'Suffolk monumental inscriptions', *Register of English Monumental Inscriptions* 2, 1914, 126-31.

PARTRIDGE, CHARLES. 'List of Suffolk churchyard inscriptions in print up to December 31st 1907', *East Anglian* N.S. **12**, 1907-8, 217.

A list of Suffolk transcripts in the British Library is in:

MARSHALL, G.W. 'Monumental inscriptions', *East Anglian* **1**, 1858-63, 431-6.

See also:

HALLIDAY, ROBERT. 'Wayside graves and crossroad burials', *Suffolk review*, N.S. **11**, 1988, 1-8. General discussion.

LINNELL, C.L.S. 'Suffolk church monuments', *S.I.A.* **27**, 1958, 1-24. Includes list of sculptors and persons commemorated.

PARTRIDGE, C.S., et al. 'Names on gravestones in Suffolk churchyards', *East Anglian* N.S. **6**, 1895-6, 134, 152-3, 166-7, 182-4, 205-6, 233, 280, 315-6, 348-9 and 367-8. In many parishes.

PROBERT, W.G.C. 'Arms and epitaphs in parish churches, chiefly of Suffolk and Essex visited by William Tyllotson between 1594 and 1600', *S.I.A.* **19**, 1927, 78-9. Description of a 16th c. transcription.

WICKHAM, A.K. 'The Jacobean country church, 3: Suffolk families', *Geographical magazine* **12**, 1940-41, 280-93. Brief general discussion.

Brasses

A number of works deal with the brass memorials of Suffolk. These include:

COTMAN, JOHN SELL. *Engravings of sepulchral brasses in Norfolk and Suffolk, tending to illustrate the ecclesiastical, military and civil costume, as well as to preserve memorials of ancient families in that county.* 2 vols. 2nd. ed. Henry G. Bohn, 1839. This work has been the subject of another book: GRIFFIN, RALPH H. *Cotman's Suffolk brasses, 1819.* Privately printed, 1937.

FARRER, EDMUND. *A list of monumental brasses remaining in the county of Suffolk, MDCCCCIII.* Norwich: Agas H. Goose, 1903. Listed by parish.

FELGATE, T.M. *Suffolk heraldic brasses.* Ipswich: East Anglian Magazine, 1978.

FELGATE, T.M. *Knights on Suffolk brasses.* Ipswich: East Anglian Magazine, 1976.

FELGATE, T.M. *Ladies on Suffolk brasses.* Ipswich: East Anglian Magazine, 1989.

Brasses *continued*

MACCULLOCH, DIARMAID. 'Suffolk brasses: a study', *Suffolk fair* **3**(8), 1974, 18-20; **3**(9), 1974, 14-17; **3**(10), 1974, 28-30 and **3**(11), 1974, 10-12. General discussion.

SPINKS, WINIFRED. *A memento from old England.* Bardwell: the author, 1977. A study of brasses in Norfolk and Suffolk, etc.

'Collection of brass rubbings in the possession of the Suffolk Institute of Archaeology', *S.I.A.* **10**, 1900, 237-49. List.

BLATCHLY, J.M. 'The lost cross brasses of Suffolk, 1320-1420', *Transactions of the Monumental Brass Society* **12**, 1974, 21-45.

MANDER, R.P. 'East Anglian brasses', *East Anglian Magazine* **6**(7), 1947, 340-6. See also 456-7. Brief note.

Heraldry

Much information on Suffolk heraldry is in print. For a modern introduction, see:

REYNOLDS, G. DAVID & MACLACHLAN, PETER, eds. *Guide to heraldry in Suffolk churches.* Great Yarmouth: Suffolk Heraldry Society, 1990.

Detailed heraldic information from many of the county's churches is provided in:

SUFFOLK HERALDRY SOCIETY. *The heraldry of Suffolk churches.* 51 vols. to date. Ipswich: the Society, 1974–See also:

SPERLING, JOHN H. 'A visitation of the monumental heraldry of Suffolk', *East Anglian* **1**, 1858-63, 105-6, 135-6, 257-8, 311-13 and 395-8.

For hatchments, see:

SUMMERS, PETER. *Hatchments in Britain, vol.2: Norfolk and Suffolk.* Phillimore, 1976.

SUMMERS, P.G. 'Funeral hatchments in Suffolk', *S.I.A.* **26**, 1955, 208-13. See also **27**, 1958, 58.

Other heraldic works are listed above, Section 5.

B. BY PLACE

Akenham

L., H.R. 'Akenham church', *E.A.M.* **1957**, passim. Monumental inscriptions.

Aldeburgh

PARTRIDGE, C. 'Aldeburgh inscriptions', *E.A.M.* **1915**, 2-3, 5, 6, 11, 12 and 24.

Aldham

PARTRIDGE, C. 'Churchyard inscriptions from Aldham, in the Hundred of Cosford and county of Suffolk, 1901', *Register of monumental inscriptions* **1**, 1911, 35-7.

Alpheton

'Inscriptions in Alpheton churchyard', *E.A.M.* **1913**, 94, 98, 101-2 and 109; **1914**, 4 and 21.

Ampton

PAGE, AUGUSTINE. 'Ampton church', *Proceedings of the Bury and West Suffolk Archaeological Institute* **1**, 1853, 190-98. Includes some memorial inscriptions, with list of clergy.

Barrow

GREENING, S. 'Were your forefathers buried in All Saints churchyard?', *Pagus* **3**, 1984, 7-10. Index to monumental inscriptions at Barrow.

Battisford

PARTRIDGE, CHARLES. 'Monumental inscriptions in Battisford churchyard, Suffolk', *East Anglian* N.S. **11**, 1905-6, 86-7.

Benhall

WAYMAN, H.W.B. 'Benhall, Suffolk', *E.A.M.* **1911**, 2, 4-5, 9, 11, 13-14, 16, 19, 23 and 24-5. Includes monumental inscriptions.

Blundeston

'Monumental inscriptions at Blundestone, Suffolk', *East Anglian* **4**, 1870, 199-201.

Bradfield St.George

P[ARTRIDGE], C. 'Bradfield S.George churchyard', *E.A.M.* **1933**, 89-90 and 91-2. Lists 65 monumental inscriptions.

Bredfield

NORRINGTON, VALERIE. 'Suffolk's first Quaker burial ground', *Suffolk review*, N.S. **4**, 1985, 1-7. General discussion of cemetery at Bredfield.

Brettenham

P[ARTRIDGE], C. 'Brettenham churchyard', *E.A.M.* **1933**, 40-41. Lists 28 monumental inscriptions.

Brome

A short guide to the memorials in Brome church, Suffolk, with notice of other memorials now lost, together with some few remarks about Brome families and their estates. Diss: Diss Publishing Co., 1938. Includes list of clergy and churchwardens.

Burstall

PARTRIDGE, CHARLES. 'Monumental inscriptions in Burstall churchyard, Suffolk', *East Anglian* N.S. **12**, 1907-8, 174-5.

Bury St.Edmunds

TYMMS, SAMUEL. *An architectural and historical account of the church of St.Mary, Bury St.Edmunds.* Bury St.Edmunds: Jackson & Frost, 1854. Includes monumental inscriptions, lists of clergy, etc.

Cavendish

HASLEWOOD, FRANCIS. 'Cavendish church', *S.I.A.* **8**, 1894, 263-73. Includes monumental inscriptions, list of rectors, parish register extracts, etc.

Chattisham

W., A.H. 'Monumental inscriptions on stones in Chattisham church, Co.Suffolk', *East Anglian* N.S. **5**, 1893-4, 19-20. See also N.S. **6**, 1895-6, 143.

Chillesford

WAYMAN, H.W.B. 'Chillesford, Suffolk', *E.A.M.* **1910**, 131 and 134-5. Includes monumental inscriptions.

Clare

'Heraldic notes taken at Clare in the reign of Queen Elizabeth', *Topographer and Genealogist* **2**, 1853, 398-402.

Debenham

BACON, H.F. 'Monumental inscriptions: Debenham church', *East Anglian* N.S. **1**, 1885-6, 55-7.

x. 'Debenham church inscriptions', *E.A.M.* **1916**, 57. See also 61.

Dennington

'Monumental inscriptions in Dennington Church', *S.I.A.* **8**, 1894, 77-9.

Denston

HASLEWOOD, FRANCIS. 'Monumental inscriptions in the parish of Denston, Suffolk', *S.I.A.* **6**, 1888, 407-24.

Drinkstone

CRESWELL, G.G. BAKER. 'Inscriptions and coats of arms formerly in the windows of Drinkstone church', *East Anglian* N.S. **6**, 1895-6, 5-7.

Dunwich

HASLEWOOD, FRANCIS. 'Monuments in the churchyard of All Saints, Dunwich', *S.I.A.* **7**, 1891, 253-4.

Earl Soham

'Earl Soham churchyard', *E.A.M.* **1927**, 10. List of pre-1750 monumental inscriptions.

Easton

DUNCAN, HAROLD N. & PACKARD, JOHN. *Easton All Saints church: church and churchyard inscriptions.* [J.L. Packard], [1972]. Includes list of rectors.

Easton Bevents

'The church and records of Easton Bavent', *E.A.M.* **1911**, 114. Easton Bevents.

Ellough

[CRISP, F.A., ed.] *Monumental inscriptions in the church and churchyard of Ellough, Suffolk.* F.A. Crisp, 1889.

Eye

'The church of St.Peter and St.Paul, Eye', *S.I.A.* **2**, 1859, 125-48. Includes monumental inscriptions, with list of vicars.

Fakenham Magna

P[ARTRIDGE], C. 'Fakenham Magna churchyard', *E.A.M.* **1933**, 58-9. Monumental inscriptions.

Farnham

WAYMAN, H.W.B. 'Farnham, Suffolk', *E.A.M.* **1911**, 26-7, 30-31 and 33. Includes monumental inscriptions.

Felixstowe

'Surnames found on monumental inscriptions at the Baptist Church, Maidstone Road, Felixstowe, Suffolk', *R. & B.* **1**(2), 1986, 12-19. Gives dates.

Felsham

P[ARTRIDGE], C. 'Felsham churchyard', *E.A.M.* **1942**, 1-2. Lists 18 monumental inscriptions.

Fornham St.Martin

YOUNGER, G.W. 'Notes on the church of Fornham St.Martin, Bury St.Edmunds, Suffolk', *Genealogists magazine* **6**, 1932-4, 508-9. Mainly notes on inscriptions.

Framlingham

GREEN, R. *History, topography, and antiquities of Framlingham and Saxted ... with biographical sketches ...* Whittaker Treacher & Co., 1834. Includes alphabetical list of monumental inscriptions, list of clergy and much else.

Freston

'The monumental inscriptions in the church of St.Peter at Freston in the Hundred of Samford in the county of Suffolk, 1908', *Register of English Monumental Inscriptions* **2**, 1914, 37-47.

Friston

WAYMAN, H.W.B. 'Friston, Suffolk', *E.A.M.* **1910**, 92-3, 94-5 and 99. Includes monumental inscriptions.

Gislingham

P[ARTRIDGE], C. 'Gislingham church, heraldry in', *E.A.M.* **1930**, 30-31.

Great Ashfield

'Ashfield Magna churchyard', *E.A.M.* **1933**, 8. Lists 13 monumental inscriptions at Great Ashfield.

Great Bealings

P[ARTRIDGE], C. 'Bealings Magna churchyard', *E.A.M.* **1934**, 35-6. Monumental inscriptions at Great Bealings.

Great Glemham

WAYMAN, H.W.B. 'Glemham Magna, Suffolk', *E.A.M.* **1911**, 40, 43-4, 45 and 50.

Great Waldingfield

HASLEWOOD, FRANCIS. 'Monumental inscriptions at Great Waldingfield', *S.I.A.* **9**, 1897, 102-10.

Halesworth

HASLEWOOD, FRANCIS. 'Monumental inscriptions in Halesworth church and churchyard', *S.I.A.* **9**, 1897, 234-55.

Hintlesham

PARTRIDGE, CHARLES. 'Monumental inscriptions in Hintlesham churchyard, Suffolk', *East Anglian* N.S. **11**, 1905-6, 229-31 and 252-4.

Ipswich

CORDER, JOAN & BLATCHLY, JOHN. 'Notes on the series of coats of arms below the roof of St.Margaret's Church, Ipswich', *Blazon* **36**, 1986 (unpaginated).

HASLEWOOD, FRANCIS. *The monumental inscriptions in the parish of Saint Matthew, Ipswich, Suffolk.* Ipswich: privately printed, 1884.

WODDERSPOON, J. *Memorials of the ancient town of Ipswich, in the county of Suffolk.* Ipswich: Pawsey, 1850. General history of Ipswich, but including monumental inscriptions at length.

Layham

PARTRIDGE, C. 'Churchyard inscriptions from Layham ... 1901', *Register of English Monumental Inscriptions* **1**, 1911-12, 38-46.

Leiston

P[ARTRIDGE], C. 'Leiston churchyard', *E.A.M.* **1933**, 62 and 66.

Little Livermere

P[ARTRIDGE], C. 'Livermere Parva churchyard', *E.A.M.* **1933**, 28-9. 24 monumental inscriptions at Little Livermere.

Little Waldingfield

HASLEWOOD, FRANCIS. 'Monumental inscriptions at Little Waldingfield', *S.I.A.* **9**, 1897, 122-30.

Long Melford

ALMACK, RICHARD. 'Some account of Melford church', *S.I.A.* **2**, 1859, 73-83. Monumental inscriptions, etc., with brief biographical notes.

Martlesham

GOLDING, CHARLES. 'Monumental inscriptions in Martlesham Church, Suffolk', *Eastern Counties Collectanea* 1872-3, 57-8.

Mellis

'Mellis churchyard', *E.A.M.* **1932**, 15. See also 18. Lists 20 monumental inscriptions.

Mendlesham

PARTRIDGE, CHARLES. 'Monumental inscriptions in Mendlesham churchyard, Co.Suffolk', *East Anglian* N.S. **12**,1907-8, 250-51.

Mildenhall

HESELTINE, PETER. 'Brasses and indents at Mildenhall, Suffolk', *Monumental Brass Society transactions* **12**,1978, 128-37.

Monk Soham

WAYMAN, H.W.B. 'Monk Soham, Suffolk', *E.A.M.* **1910**, 31, 33-4 and 42-3. Includes monumental inscriptions.

North Cove

'Monumental inscriptions at North Cove, Suffolk', *East Anglian* **4**, 1870, 265-9.

Old Newton

P[ARTRIDGE], C.S. 'Monumental inscriptions in Old Newton church, Suffolk', *East Anglian* N.S. **4**, 1891-2, 332-3. See also 343; N.S. **5**, 1893-4, 221-2 and 248.

P[ARTRIDGE], C. 'Old Newton churchyard', *E.A.M.* **1935**, 27-8. Lists 36 monumental inscriptions.

Orford

WAYMAN, H.W. BILLING. 'Monumental inscriptions in the church of St.Bartholomew, at Orford, Suffolk', *East Anglian* N.S. **13**, 1909-10, 66-7, 193-6 and 265.

W[AYMAN], H.W.B. 'The monumental inscriptions remaining in the church of St.Bartholomew at Orford, ... 1911', *Register of English Monumental Inscriptions* **1**, 1911, 1-34.

Poslingford

JARVIS, HENRY. 'Poslingford church', *S.I.A.* **8**, 1894, 241-56. Includes monumental inscriptions, list of vicars, etc.

Rendham

'Rendham, Suffolk', *E.A.M.* **1910**, 119-20, 122-3, 125-6 and 127-8. Includes monumental inscriptions.

Rushbrooke

DAVY, H.I. & DAVID ELISHA. 'Church notes: Rushbrooke', *S.I.A.* **7**, 1891, 336-62. Includes monumental inscriptions, list of rectors and manorial lords, parish register extracts, etc.

Saxstead

See Framlingham

Snape

WAYMAN, H.W.B. 'Snape, Suffolk', *E.A.M.* **1910**, 81, 83, 87-8 and 90-91. Includes monumental inscriptions.

Sotterley

'Monumental inscriptions at Sotterley church, Suffolk', *East Anglian* **4**, 1869-70, 289-91.

Southwold

GOODING, D.R. 'Monumental inscriptions from the graveyard of the Congregational chapel in the borough of Southwold, in the county of Suffolk, 1908', *Register of English Monumental Inscriptions* **2**, 1914, 46-7.

GOODING, D.R. 'The monumental inscriptions remaining in the churchyard of the parish church of St.Edmund, in the borough of Southwold and county of Suffolk, 1908', *Register of English Monumental Inscriptions* **2**,1913-14, 104-14.

LINGWOOD, A.R. 'Inscriptions in Southwold churchyard', *E.A.M.* **1913**, 75, 78 and 83.

Sternfield

WAYMAN, H.W.B. 'Sternfield, Suffolk', *E.A.M.* **1910**, 101-2, 103-4, 106-7, 109 and 112. Includes monumental inscriptions.

Stoke Ash

SEWELL, W.H. 'On the parish and parish church of All Saints, Stoke Ash', *S.I.A.* **4**, 1863, 417-43. Includes monumental inscriptions, list of rectors, and list of manorial lords.

Stoke by Nayland

Inscriptions in Stoke by Nayland churchyard, Suffolk. Harrison & Sons, 1877.

'Stoke by Nayland church', *S.I.A.* **4**, 1863, 183-207. Includes some monumental inscriptions, with descents of manors, list of vicars, and will of John de Payton, 1318.

Stratford St.Andrew

WAYMAN, H.W.B. 'Stratford St.Andrew, Suffolk', *E.A.M.* **1910**, 20-21 and 25-6.

Stutton

CRISP, FREDERICK ARTHUR. *Some account of the parish of Stutton, near Ipswich in the county of Suffolk*. F.A. Crisp, 1881. Includes monumental inscriptions, extracts from parish registers, list of clergy, etc.

Sudbury

PARTRIDGE, CHARLES. 'Friends memorials at Sudbury', *E.A.M.* **1954**, 3 and 4. Lists 34 monumental inscriptions.

Sweffling

WAYMAN, H.W. BILLING. 'Monumental inscriptions in Sweffling, Co.Suffolk', *East Anglian* N.S. **12**, 1906-7, 134-6 and 155-7.

W[AYMAN], H.W.B. 'The monumental inscriptions remaining in the church and churchyard at Swefling, in the Hundred of Plomesgate in the county of Suffolk, 1907', *Register of English Monumental Inscriptions* **1**, 1911, 47-54.

Trimley

FELIXSTOWE FAMILY HISTORY SOCIETY. *A record of the monumental inscriptions of the churchyards of Trimley, Ipswich, Suffolk*. Felixstowe: the Society, 1987.

Tuddenham St.Martin

RICHARDSON, W.H. 'Monumental inscriptions from Tuddenham Church, Co.Suffolk', *M.G.H.* N.S. **3**, 1880, 204-5.

Tunstall

'Tunstall, Suffolk', *E.A.M.* **1910**, 65-6, 68, 71, 73-4 and 79. Includes monumental inscriptions.

Ufford

P[ARTRIDGE], C., & D., H. *Inscriptions in Ufford churchyard, Suffolk, also names of those buried in the New Churchyard without tombstones.* [Ufford?]: [ ], 1931?

Walpole

P[ARTRIDGE], C. 'Walpole churchyard', *E.A.M.* **1932**, 69. Notes 33 monumental inscriptions.

Wantisden

W[AYMAN], H.W.B. 'The monumental inscriptions remaining in the church at Wantisden in the hundred of Plomesgate, in the county of Suffolk, 1907', *Register of Monumental Inscriptions* **1**, 1911, 55-61.

Wantisden *continued*

'Monumental inscriptions within the church and churchyard of Wantisden, Co.Suffolk', *East Anglian* N.S. **12**, 1906-7, 66-8.

Westley

P[ARTRIDGE], C. 'Westley churchyard', *E.A.M.* **1934**, 30-31. 21 monumental inscriptions.

Worlingham

'Monumental inscriptions in Worlingham church, Suffolk', *East Anglian* **4**, 1870, 207-9 and 225-6.

Yoxford

HASLEWOOD, FRANCIS. 'Notes on Yoxford church, transcribed from the collections of Davy with additions (British Museum Add. ms. 19, 083, 262)', *S.I.A.* **8**, 1894, 39-50. Includes monumental inscriptions, list of vicars, etc.

Stray memorials

A number of works list Suffolk memorials found in other counties, and memorials from other counties found in Suffolk:

'Monumental inscriptions relating to East Anglia from other counties', *East Anglian* N.S. **2-11**, 1887/8-1905/6, passim.

PARTRIDGE, C. 'Suffolk churchyard inscriptions relating to other counties and countries', *Notes and queries* **150**, 1926, 222-3, 313 and 421-2; **151**, 1926, 8-9, 76-7, 149-50 and 241-2.

PARTRIDGE, CHARLES. 'Essex inscriptions in Suffolk churchyards', *Essex review* **35**, 1926, 144-8; **45**, 1936, 174-7 and 239-42; **46**, 1937, 109-12 and 170-2.

'Suffolk monumental inscriptions in the city of Norwich', *East Anglian* N.S. **2**, 1887-8, 84-6, 101-3 and 198-200.

C. *BY FAMILY*

Alington

BARTRUM, H.H. 'The Alington tomb at Milden, 1627', *E.A.M.* **1909**, 106.

Alvard

See Wimbill

Appleton

A[PPLETON], J. *Monumental memorials of the Appleton family*. Boston, Mass.: privately printed, 1867. Includes brief biographical notes.

Arundel

BENT, J. THEODORE. 'The tombs at Chilton', *Antiquary* **5**, 1882, 59-60. Of Lady Arundel, 1508, and Sir Robert Crane, 1643.

Barnardiston

W., L.H.H. 'The vaults at Kedington', *E.A.M.* **1933**, 14, 15 and 17. Barnardiston family monumental inscriptions.

'Barnardiston vaults in Kedington church', *S.I.A.* **16**, 1918, 44-8. Includes parish register extracts.

Boteler

MANNING, C.R. 'A sepulchral monument at Newton by Sudbury', *S.I.A.* **9**, 1897, 262-70. Probably of Margaret Boteler, 1410. Includes medieval pedigrees of Boteler and Carbonell.

Bovile

BLATCHLY, JOHN. 'The lost and mutilated memorials of the Bovile and Wingfield families at Letheringham', *S.I.A.* **33**, 1976, 168-94. Includes pedigree, 14-17th c.

Brayles

S., J.H. & CASLEY, H.C. 'A Suffolk brass', *Antiquary* **8**, 1883, 135 and 242-3. To John Brayles, 1464; includes his will.

Carbonell
See Butler

Crane
See Arundel

Crosyer

CAMERON, H.K. & PAGE-PHILLIPS, J.C. 'The brass of John Crosyer at Barrow, Suffolk', *Monumental Brass Society transactions* **13**(3), 1982, 224-31. 16th c.

De Vere

DEWING, E.M. 'Further notes upon Lavenham church', *S.I.A.* **6**, 1888, 225-35. Notes on the heraldry of the De Vere family, with a pedigree.

D'Ewes

'The monumental brasses to the infant son of Sir Simonds D'Ewes in Lavenham church', *East Anglian* N.S. **8**, 1899-1900, 49-50. 1628.

Fairclough

PARTRIDGE, CHARLES. 'Fairclough family of Stowmarket', *East Anglian* N.S. **11**, 1905-6, 207-8. Monumental inscriptions.

Fowle

DOW, LESLIE. 'An armorial shield at Shrubland Park', *S.I.A.* **27**, 1958, 123-4. Of Fowle impaling Mingay; includes genealogical notes, 17-19th c.

Garnham

'Garnham of Suffolk', *East Anglian* N.S. **8**, 1899-1900, 41-2. Monumental inscriptions.

Hammond

PEARSON, WILLIAM C. 'The Hammond vault in Whitton church, Suffolk', *East Anglian* N.S. **9**, 1901-2, 346-8. Monumental inscriptions, includes parish register extracts.

Hervey

HERVEY, ARTHUR. 'Sir Nicholas Hervey, Kt.', *S.I.A.* **3**, 1863, 315-20. Brass, early 16th c.

Howard

EDWARDS, GEORGE OCTAVIUS. 'Notes on the Howard monument in the south aisle of Framlingham church', *S.I.A.* **3**, 1864, 352-7.

MARKS, RICHARD. 'The Howard tombs at Thetford and Framlingham: new discoveries', *Archaeological journal* **141**, 1985, 252-68. Includes pedigree, 15-16th c.

STONE, LAWRENCE & COLVIN, HOWARD. 'The Howard tomb at Framlingham, Suffolk', *Archaeological journal* **122**, 1965, 159-71.

Keble

MUSKETT, J.J. 'The Keble arms in Tuddenham church, Suffolk', *East Anglian* N.S. **11**, 1905-6, 241.

Kemball

A., T. 'Kemball of Suffolk', *East Anglian* N.S. **6**, 1895-6, 366-7. Monumental inscriptions.

Kerridge

PARTRIDGE, CHARLES S. 'Kerridge of Shelley Hall, Suffolk', *East Anglian* N.S. **6**, 1895-6, 89-91. Monumental inscriptions.

Martin

P[ARTRIDGE], C.S. 'Martin of Suffolk', *East Anglian* N.S. **5**, 1893-4, 87. Monumental inscriptions, 18th c.

Mingay
See Fowle

Nayler

'Nayler of Icklingham', *E.A.M.* **1928**, 15 and 16. Monumental inscriptions.

Peyton

BLATCHLY, JOHN. 'The Peyton indents at Stoke-by-Nayland', *Transactions of the Monumental Brass Society* **11**, 1973, 382. 14th c.

EVANS, H.F. OWEN. 'Peyton slabs at Stoke-by-Nayland', *Transactions of the Monumental Brass Society* **10**, 1963-8, 13-15. 14th c.

Monumental Inscriptions: By Family *continued*

Prior

'Prior of Timworth', *E.A.M.* **1932**, 23. Mainly monumental inscriptions.

Ranson

W., L.H.H. 'Ranson family tomb inscriptions', *E.A.M.* **1931**, passim.

Rous

GREEN, E. 'Monumental inscriptions to the family of Rous in Wangford church, Co.Suffolk', *Genealogist* N.S. **19**, 1902, 97-100.

Rush

See Wimbill

Savage

DOW, LESLIE. 'The Savage hatchment at Long Melford', *S.I.A.* **26**, 1955, 214-7. Viscount Savage, 1635.

Stubbin

PARTRIDGE, C.S. 'Stubbin of Raydon and Higham, Suffolk', *East Anglian* N.S. **4**, 1891-2, 245 and **5**, 1893-4, 69-70. Monumental inscriptions and parish register extracts.

Talboys

CHRISTIAN, J.A. 'Identifying the brasses at Assington, Suffolk', *Transactions of the Monumental Brass Society* **11**, 1975, 431-6. Probably Talboys family, early 16th c.

Tendryng

BLATCHLY, JOHN & NORTHEAST, PETER. 'The Tendryng brass at Holbrook, Suffolk', *Monumental Brass Society transactions* **13**, 1985, 484-9. Includes pedigree showing descent of Elizabeth Tendryng from Holbrooke and Wolverstone, 14-15th c.

Tye

BLATCHLY, JOHN. 'The much-attributed military brass at Barsham, Suffolk', *Transactions of the Monumental Brass Society* **14**(1), 1986, 39-43. Attributed to Sir Robert de Tye, died 1415.

Vernon

CULLUM, GERY MILNER GIBSON. 'Cullum', *M.G.H.* 2nd series, **4**, 1892, 203-7. Monumental inscriptions relating to the Vernon family; includes pedigree, 18-19th c.

Ward

PARTRIDGE, CHARLES S. 'Ward of Old Newton, Suffolk', *East Anglian* N.S. **5**, 1893-4, 150-51. See also 158-9. Monumental inscriptions.

Whimper

'Whimper of Suffolk', *E.A.M.* **1932**, 51-2. See also 81. Monumental inscriptions.

Wimbill

MACCULLOCH, DIARMAID. 'Recent discoveries at St.Stephens Church, Ipswich: the Wimbill chancel and the Rush-Alvard chancel', *S.I.A.* **36**(2), 1986, 101-14. Includes pedigree showing relationship of Wimbill, Rush and Alvard, 16th c.

Wingfield

BLATCHLY, J.M. & GREENWOOD, J. ROGER. 'A Norwich-style brass to three Wingfield brothers, once at Letheringham, Suffolk', *Monumental Brass Society transactions* **12**,1978, 300-11. Includes pedigree, 15th c., and will of William Wingfield, 1509/10.
See also Bovile

Withipoll

MACCULLOCH, D.N.J. & BLATCHLY, J.M. 'An Ipswich conundrum: the Withipoll memorials', *Monumental Brass Society transactions* **12**,1977, 240-7.

Wollaston

P[ARTRIDGE], C. 'Wollaston of Finborough', *E.A.M.* **1933**, 4-5. Monumental inscriptions.

Woodthorpe

BENTON, G.M. 'Brass of Agnes Woodthorpe, S.Peter's church, Colchester', *Essex Archaeological Society transactions* N.S. **13**, 1913-14, 309-10. See also N.S. **15**, 1918-20, 156. Discusses a duplicate commemoration at Lavenham.

10. PROBATE RECORDS

Probate records are invaluable sources of genealogical information: most wills list all living children; other relatives are often mentioned, as are places with which the testator has been associated. An authoritative summary of probate jurisdiction in Suffolk before 1858 is to be found in:

GIBSON, J.S.W. 'Probate jurisdiction in Suffolk before 1858', *S.Rt.* **4**(2), 1978, 22-3.

Suffolk was in the diocese of Norwich; most wills were proved in the courts of the Archdeacons of Sudbury and Suffolk. Some, however, are to be found in the records of the Norwich Consistory Court; these are indexed in:

FARROW, M.A., ed. *Index to wills proved in the Consistory Court of Norwich and now preserved in the district probate registry at Norwich, 1370-1550, and wills among the Norwich enrolled deeds, 1286-1508.* Index Library, **69**, 1945. Also issued as Norfolk Record Society, **16**, 1944 (the title page of the latter gives 1298 instead of 1286).

FARROW, M.A. *Index to wills proved in the Consistory Court of Norwich ... 1550-1603.* Norfolk Record Society, **21**, 1950. Also published as Index Library, **73**. Includes many Suffolk wills.

FARROW, M.A. & BARTON, T.F., eds. *Index of wills proved in the consistory court of Norwich and now preserved in the District Probate Registry at Norwich, 1604-1686.* Norfolk Record Society, **28**, 1958.

BARTON, THOMAS F. & FARROW, M.A., eds. *Index of wills proved in the Consistory Court of Norwich, 1687-1750, and now preserved in the Norfolk and Norwich Record Office.* Norfolk Record Society, **34**, 1965.

BARTON, THOMAS F., FARROW, M.A. & BEDINGFELD, A.L. *Index of wills proved in the Consistory Court of Norwich, 1751-1818, and now preserved in the Norfolk and Norwich Record Office.* Norfolk Record Society, **38**, 1969.

FROSTICK, CLAIRE. *Index of wills proved in the Consistory Court of Norwich, 1819-1857, and now preserved in the Norfolk Record Office.* Norfolk Record Society, **47**, 1980.

Probate records from the Archdeaconry of Sudbury are listed or abstracted in a number of works:

GRIMWADE, M.E. *Index of the probate records of the court of the Archdeacon of Sudbury, 1354-1700.* ed. W.R. and R.K. Serjeant. 2 vols. Index Library, 95-6. British Record Society, 1986.

TYMMS, SAMUEL, ed. *Wills and inventories from the registers of the commissary of Bury St.Edmunds and the Archdeacon of Sudbury.* Camden Society old series, **49**, 1850. A selection, 1370-1650, made to illustrate the customs and language of the period, rather than genealogy.

EVANS, NESTA, ed. *The wills of the Archdeaconry of Sudbury, 1630-1635.* S.R.S., **29**. Woodbridge: Boydell Press, 1987.

CHRISTIE, PETER. 'Some newly discovered Suffolk and Cambridgeshire probate inventories', *S.Rt.* **2**(2), 1976, 14-15. List of 38 inventories from the Archdeaconry of Sudbury, presumably used as evidence in cases of disputed wills, and previously unlisted.

The probate records of the Archdeaconry of Suffolk are dealt with in:

REDSTONE, VINCENT B. *Calendar of pre-Reformation wills, testaments, probates, administrations registered at the Probate Office, Bury St.Edmunds.* Ipswich: W.E. Harrison, 1907. Covers 1354-1535; has many inaccuracies.

See also:

PARTRIDGE, CHARLES. 'Tabular lists from Mr. Redstone's calendar of Bury wills', *S.I.A.* **13**, 1909, 57-107.

GRIMWADE, M.E. *Index of the probate records of the court of the archdeacon of Suffolk, 1444-1700.* ed. W.R. and R.K. Serjeant. 2 vols. Index Library, **90-91**. British Record Society, 1979-80.

CRISP, F.A. *Calendar of wills at Ipswich, 1440-1600.* Privately printed, 1895. Index only.

LAYTON, W.E. 'Calendar of early Suffolk wills, Ipswich registry, A.D.1444-1620', *East Anglian* N.S. **5**, 1893-4, 62-3, 110-11, 156-7, 218-9, 277-9 and 332-4.

'Calendar of early Suffolk wills, Ipswich registry, A.D.1444-1620', *East Anglian* N.S. **1**, 1885-6; **2**, 1887-8, passim.

ALLEN, MARION E., ed. *Wills of the Archdeaconry of Suffolk, 1620-1624.* S.R.S., **31**. Woodbridge: Boydell Press, 1989. Includes 784 wills.

ALLEN, MARION E. & EVANS, NESTA R., eds. *Wills from the Archdeaconry of Suffolk, 1629-1636.* Boston, Mass.: New England Historic Genealogical Society, 1986. Detailed abstracts. A further volume covers 1637-1640.

Suffolk wills in the Prerogative Court of Canterbury are listed in:

OSWALD-HICKS, T.W., ed. *A calendar of wills relating to the county of Suffolk proved in the Prerogative Court of Canterbury between 1383 and 1604.* Poole and Pemberton, 1913.

For some omissions from this list, see:
BULLEN, R. FREEMAN. 'Suffolk wills 1500-01',
   E.A.M. **1943**, 4, 6, 8, 9, 11 and 12.
Many other Suffolk wills were proved in the
Prerogative Court of Canterbury. Indexes and
calendars to these wills are listed in my *English
genealogy: an introductory bibliography*.
A list of Suffolk wills, 14-17th c., in the British
Library is printed in:
BULLEN, R. FREEMAN. 'Suffolk wills in the British
   Museum', *E.A.M.* **1913**, 70-71. Lists, 14-17th c.
A discussion of the contents of the Suffolk Record
Society volumes listed above is to be found in:
SERJEANT, RUTH. 'The making of the Suffolk will
   index', *Suffolk review*, N.S. **3**, 1984, 11-14.
Extracts from 11 16-17th c. Suffolk wills are
given in:
BARROW, GEOFFREY B. 'Some Suffolk wills',
   Genealogical quarterly **40**, 1973-4, 3-5.
A number of collections and indexes of probate
records relating to particular places have been
published. These include:

Bocking Deanery

EMMISON, F.G., ed. *Index to wills at Chelmsford
   (Essex and East Hertfordshire)*. Index Library,
   79 and **84**. British Record Society, 1961-9.
   Vol.2 1620-1720. Vol.3 1721-1858. Bocking
   Deanery includes Hadleigh, Monks Eleigh and
   Moulton, all in Suffolk. Vol.1 does not include
   wills from Bocking.

Bury St.Edmunds

BULLEN, R. FREEMAN. 'Index to Bury wills in the
   Prerogative Court of Canterbury, 1383-1604',
   East Anglian N.S. **13**, 1909-10, 116-21.
BULLEN, R. FREEMAN. 'Index to Bury wills in the
   Prerogative Court of Canterbury, 1406 to 1558',
   E.A.M. **1910**, 22-3 and 24-5.
BULLEN, R. FREEMAN. 'Bury wills, 1630-1651',
   E.A.M. **1913**, 42, 44 and 46. In the Prerogative
   Court of Canterbury.

Coney Weston

WILKINSON, B. 'The poore of the parish', *Local
   historian* **16**, 1984, 21-3. Coney Weston,
   Suffolk; discusses legacies to the poor.

Eriswell

MUNDAY, J.T. *Twelve Eriswell wills, 1500-1545*.
   Brandon: the author, 1965.

Haverhill

CROUCH, PATRICK. 'Haverhill probate inventories',
   Haverhill historian **2**(5-10), 1984-7, passim.

Ipswich

REDSTONE, VINCENT B. 'Early Suffolk wills', *S.I.A.*
   15, 1915, 291-304. Calendar of wills enrolled in
   the records of Ipswich Corporation, 1254-1660.
REED, MICHAEL, ed. *The Ipswich probate
   inventories, 1583-1631*. S.R.S., **22**. Ipswich:
   Boydell Press, 1981. Transcripts of the earliest
   72 inventories for Ipswich from the
   Archdeaconry of Suffolk and the Norwich
   Consistory Court.

Ixworth

TYMMS, SAMUEL. 'Wills and extracts from wills
   relating to Ixworth and Ixworth Thorpe',
   *Proceedings of the Bury and West Suffolk
   Archaeological Institute* **1**, 1853, 103-20. Wills
   of 16 testators.

Lakenheath

MUNDAY, J.T., ed. *Thirty testaments*. Lakenheath
   records, **3**. Lakenheath: J.T. Munday, 1969.
   Wills of Lakenheath, 1404-1538, with 1523 lay
   subsidy.

Newmarket

MAY, PETER. *Newmarket inventories, 1662-1715*.
   Newmarket: the author, 1976.
MAY, PETER. *Twenty Newmarket wills, 1439-1497:
   a glimpse of fifteenth century Newmarket*. Bury
   St.Edmunds: Suffolk Bookshop, 1974.

Orford

W[AYMAN], H.W.B., ed. *Suffolk wills (Orford) proved
   in the Prerogative Court of Canterbury between
   1383 and 1800*. Poole and Pemberton, for the
   English Monumental Inscriptions Society,
   1911.

Shotley

H[ERVEY], S.H.A. *Shotley parish records: with
   illustrations, maps and pedigrees*. S.G.B. **16**(2).
   Bury St.Edmunds: Paul & Mathew, 1912.
   Includes transcripts of 83 wills, together with
   inquisitions post mortem, tax lists, feet of fines,
   pedigrees, lists of clergy, etc.

Sibton

HASLEWOOD, FRANCIS. 'Wills from the probate
   registry at Ipswich', *S.I.A.* **8**, 1894, 63-4. From
   Sibton, 1464-1512.

South Elmham

EVANS, NESTA. 'Testators, literacy, education and
   religious belief', *Local population studies* **25**,
   1980, 42-50. Based on wills from South
   Elmham, 1550-1640.
REDSTONE, V.B. 'South Elmham Deanery', *S.I.A.*
   14, 1912, 323-30. Includes brief abstracts from
   36 wills proved in the Deanery Court, early
   16th c.

Many individual wills and inventories have been published; they are listed here by surname:

Adams
B., E.R. 'Will of Susanna Adams of Bury, 1696', *E.A.M.* **1928**, 47.

Ager
M., R.W. 'Will of Thomas Ager, 1651', *E.A.M.* **1909**, 52.

Andrew
SMITH, CHAS. 'Will of Richard Andrew, 1506', *E.A.M.* **1908**, 35.

Bacon
BULLEN, R. FREEMAN. 'Will of Isabel Bacon, 1552', *E.A.M.* **1910**, 133.

LAYTON, W.E. 'Bacon wills (from Ipswich registry)', *M.G.H.* 2nd series **2**, 1888, 284-6, 310-11, 334-6, 340-3, 357-60 and 377-8; **3**, 1890, 9-11, 22-3, 83-6, 99-100, 121-2, 135-6 and 153; **4**, 1892, 298-302, 310-11, 335-6 and 343-5; **5**, 1894, 20, 37-8, 59, 69-71, 100-102, 285-7, 308-9, 346-8 and 374-6; 3rd series **4**, 1902, 22-6 and 70-74.

'Will of Sir Nicholas Bacon, the Lord Keeper, 1578', *E.A.M.* **1933**, 15, 16-17, 21, 74 and 80.

Baker
'Will of William Baker of Stanton, 1766', *E.A.M.* **1926**, 51.

Ball
P[ARTRIDGE], C. 'Will of William Ball of Higham, 1557', *E.A.M.* **1933**, 77-8.

Balls
See Freeman

Barker
B., A. 'Will of Rev. Robert Barker of Mellis, 1747', *E.A.M.* **1916**, 76.

Beylham
BENTON, G. MONTAGU. 'Will of John Beylham of Stratford St.Mary, 1500', *E.A.M.* **1937**, 22 and 25-6.

Bixley
BIXLEY, PHILIP, ed. 'Extracts from the will of Richard Bixley, singleman, of Badingham, 1611', *S.Rt.* **12**(4), 1986, 95-6.

Blatchley
'A page for the genealogist: wills', *Pagus* **18**, 1986, 4-5. Includes will of Edwin Blatchley, 1914.

Blobold
B., A. 'Will of William Blobold of Mendham, 1625', *E.A.M.* **1916**, 88 and 97.

Blomfeild
'Will of William Blomfeild of Stonham Aspall, 1678', *E.A.M.* **1908**, 32-3.

Blosse
'Will of Joan Blosse of Ipswich, 1611', *E.A.M.* **1922**, 19.

Blowers
M., S.M.W. & MORLEY, CLAUDE. 'An inventory of 1693', *E.A.M.* **1953**, 32-3, 33-4 and 35. Thomas Blowers of Barking, Suffolk.

Bohun
F., E. 'Will of Richard Bohun, 1495', *E.A.M.* **1933**, 88.

Bokenham
B., A. 'Will of Walsingham Bokenham, 1714', *E.A.M.* **1920**, 62-3.

Boret
MORLEY, CLAUDE. 'Will of Alayn Boret, of Brundish, 1511', *E.A.M.* **1917**, 46-7 and 50.

Bradstreet
B., A. 'Will of Robert Bradstreet of Cretingham, 1616', *E.A.M.* **1920**, 81, 84, 86, 88, 89-90 and 92.

Brende
S., F.H. 'Will of Sir John Brende', *E.A.M.* **1908**, 52-3. 1559.

'Will of John Brende of Fressingfield, 1551', *E.A.M.* **1934**, 36.

Bulbrook
'Will of John Bulbrook of Tostock, 1635', *E.A.M.* **1907**, 83. See also 97-8.

Bullin
BULLEN, R. FREEMAN. 'Will of John Bullin, 1606', *E.A.M.* **1921**, 45 and 51.

BULLEN, R. FREEMAN. 'Will of Rose Bullyn, Bury, 1611', *E.A.M.* **1922**, 26.

B[ULLEN], R.F. 'Will of John Bullinge (1624)', *E.A.M.* **1914**, 50-51.

Burrough
'Wills of the Burrough family', *E.A.M.* **1932**, 58; **1933**, 7 and 13.

Cardinal
'Will of Will. Cardinal, 1595', *E.A.M.* **1909**, 26.

Chaplin

LIVETT, R.G. CHAPLIN. 'The goods of a Suffolk parson in the seventeenth century', *East Anglian* N.S. **10**, 1903-4, 33-6. Inventory of Abraham Chaplin, 1679.

Charles

'Will of Roger Charles of Beccles, 1506', *E.A.M.* **1907**, 52.

Clere

BULLEN, R. FREEMAN. 'Will of Edmund Clere of Ampton, 1521', *E.A.M.* **1913**, 34-5.

Cobbe

B., A. 'Will of George Cobbe of Mellis, 1689', *E.A.M.* **1916**, 83.

Coke

STEER, FRANCIS W. 'The inventory of Arthur Coke of Bramfield, 1629', *S.I.A.* **25**, 1952, 264-87. Includes a useful introduction and glossary of terms.

Conningesby

'The will of a Suffolk friend of Master Justice Clench, A.D.1591', *E.A.M.* **1907**, 25-6. Will of Richard Conningesby of Harkstead.

Cooke

B., A. 'Will of Jonathan Cooke of Wetheringsett, 1739', *E.A.M.* **1921**, 75.

Cornwallis

F., E. 'Will of Sir William Cornwallis, 1611', *E.A.M.* **1934**, 38-9, 48-9 and 50-1. Of Brome.
'Cornwallis wills', *East Anglian* N.S. **10**, 1903-4, 221-5. 16th c.

Crabb

SPERLING, C.F.D. 'A Suffolk yeoman's goods, 1691', *East Anglian* N.S. **5**, 1893-4, 74. Inventory of John Crabb, of Barking, Suffolk.

Dade

O., S.E. 'Will of Thomas Dade of Petistree, 1686', *E.A.M.* **1908**, 41.
'Will of John Dade, 1565', *E.A.M.* **1908**, 48. Of Ilketshall.
O., S.E. 'Will of Anne Dade, 1692', *E.A.M.* **1908**, 46. Of Pettistry.

Danyell

'Will of John Danyell the elder, 1507', *East Anglian* **2**, 1866, 281.

Darby

M., R.W. 'Will of Mary Darby, 1646', *E.A.M.* **1911**, 5-6.

Davie

B., A. 'Will of John Davie of Debenham, 1717', *E.A.M.* **1921**, 28, 29-30, 31, 33 and 38.

Daye

'A country parson of 1627', *East Anglian* N.S. **10**, 1903-4, 81-2. Will of John Daye of Little Thurlow, 1627.

De la Pole

M., R.W. 'Delapole wills', *E.A.M.* **1930**, 84. Will of Richard De La Pole, 1403.

Devereaux

P[ARTRIDGE], C. 'Will of Mary Devereaux of Old Newton, 1705', *E.A.M.* **1928**, 44 and 45.

Dowsing

M., J.J. 'The will of William Dowsing, Parliamentary Visitor to the Suffolk churches, 1643-4', *East Anglian* N.S. **1**, 1885-6, 138. 1667.

Drayles

'The will of John Drayles of the parish of St.Mary Tower', *E.A.M.* **1907**, 9-10. 1464.

Drewe

'Walton will, 1449', *R. & B.* **5**(2), 1990, 21. Will of John Drewe.

Duncan

L., H.R. 'Will of Elizabeth Dunkon of Ipswich, 1692', *E.A.M.* **1937**, 79.
L., H.R. 'Will of Elizabeth Duncon of Sproughton, 1645', *E.A.M.* **1937**, 69-70.
'Robert Dunkon of Ipswich, d.1670', *E.A.M.* **1942**, 31-2, 33, 35, 36 and 38. Will.

Estow

'Will of Edmund Estow of Woodbridge, 1675', *E.A.M.* **1932**, 8-9 and 11-12.

Euston

See Trumpoor

Everard

See Felton

Exelby

'Exelby family', *M.G.H.* 2nd series **5**, 1894, 224. Will of Miles Exelby of Stoke by Nayland, 1616.

Fairfax

'Fairfax wills of Norfolk and Suffolk', *Northern genealogist* **1**, 1895, 49-53. Includes extracts from parish registers and marriage licences.

Felton

BROWNE, A.L. 'Lady Elizabeth Felton and her daughter', *S.I.A.* **22**,1935, 170-77. Includes wills of Lady Elizabeth Felton, 1639, and Lade Anne Everard, 1653 (she died 1657).

'Will of Mary Felton of Shotley, A.D.1602', *East Anglian* N.S. **3**, 1889-90, 281-2.

Ffarrar

M., J.J. 'Will of Richard Ffarrar of Cratfield, 1651', *E.A.M.* **1908**, 122.

Field

P[ARTRIDGE], C. 'Yeoman's household goods, 1789', *E.A.M.* **1934**, 27-8, 29, 33, 34 and 36. Inventory of John Field.

Fiske

'The Fiske family papers', *E.A.M.* **1909**, 55-6. Will abstracts, 18th c.

Foorth

BULLEN, R. FREEMAN. 'I.P.M. of William Foorth of Hadleigh, 1505', *E.A.M.* **1918**, 62, 65 and 69. An inquisition post mortem, rather than a will.

Fowle

'Will of Edmund Fowle of Redgrave, 1700', *E.A.M.* **1920**, 99-100.

Fox

F., E. 'Will of Robert Fox of Fressingfield', *E.A.M.* **1934**, 5.

Freeman

'Chattels of the very poor, 1682', *E.A.M.* **1941**, 27. Inventories of Robert Freeman and Elizabeth Balls, of Great Blakenham.

Gardener

'Will of John Gardener of Bury, 1506', *Proceedings of the Bury and West Suffolk Institute of Archaeology* **1**, 1853, 329-30.

Gaudy

P[ARTRIDGE], C. 'Will of Sir Clippesby Gaudy of Wenham Parva, 1619', *E.A.M.* **1933**, 89. i.e. Little Wenham.

Geater

L., H.R. 'Will of Frances Geater, 1778', *E.A.M.* **1926**, 29 and 30-31.

Gibon

'Will of William Gibon of Ipswich, 1502', *E.A.M.* **1908**, 70.

Godell

'Will of William Godell, Southwold, 1509', *E.A.M.* **1918**, 2-3 and 12-13.

Godell *continued*

'Will of William Godell of Southwold, 1509', *E.A.M.* **1929**, 36, 37, 38-9 and 49-50.

Godfrey

'Will of John Godfrey, 1621', *E.A.M.* **1907**, 15. Of Horringer.

Gooch

'Will of Dorothy Gooch, 1811', *E.A.M.* **1912**, 118.

Goodying

REDSTONE, V.B. 'Will of Roger Goodyng of Iken, 1476', *E.A.M.* **1936**, 95.

Grene

'Will of Agnes de Grene of Fressingfield, 1435', *E.A.M.* **1934**, 3.

Grenlinge

'Will of Elizabeth Grenlinge, 1580', *E.A.M.* **1934**, 8. See also 11.

Gyrlyng

RAYSON, G. 'Old wills, no. VI: Agnes Gyrlyng, of Fressingfield, Suffolk, 1521', *East Anglian* **4**, 1869-70, 47.

'Will of Agnes Gyrlyng of Fressingfield, 1521', *E.A.M.* **1911**, 69-70.

Harvey

'Will of John Harvey of Old Newton, 1679', *E.A.M.* **1928**, 29-30.

M., R.W. 'Will of Nicholas Harvey, 1649', *E.A.M.* **1908**, 75-6.

Harwell

See Smith

Hatfield

B., A. 'Will of John Hatfield of Elmswell, 1666', *E.A.M.* **1917**, 70-71.

'Will of David Hatfield of Elmswell, 1676', *E.A.M.* **1917**, 75.

Havers

'Will of Margaret Havers', *E.A.M.* **1908**, 82-3.

Hayles

GOLDING, C. 'Will of William Hayles the elder, of Sutton in Suffolk', *East Anglian* **3**, 1866-8, 293-5. 1624.

Hayward

S., F.H. 'Will of Stephen Hayward, 1520', *E.A.M.* **1908**, 124-5.

'Will of Stephen Hayward, (1520)', *E.A.M.* **1909**, 9-10. See also 15-16.

Hervey

'Curious nuncupative will of Robert Hervey, 1599', *East Anglian* N.S. **2**, 1887-8, 83. 1599.

Heryng

TYMMS, SAMUEL. 'Will of Jone Heryng, 1419', *Proceedings of the Bury and West Suffolk Archaeological Institute* **1**, 1853, 165-6.

Heyward

Z. 'Will of William Heyward of Acton, 1552', *E.A.M.* **1940**, 9 and 10.

Hoo

S., F.H. 'Hoo wills, 1512-1521', *E.A.M.* **1907**, 46.

S., F.H. 'Will of John Hoo, 1494', *E.A.M.* **1907**, 41.

S., F.H. 'Will of Margaret Hoo, 1498', *E.A.M.* **1907**, 36.

Irby

'Will of Estelyne Irby of Thetford, 1505', *E.A.M.* **1909**, 49.

Jacob

BAINES, JOHN S. 'The Mills family', *E.A.M.* **1910**, 46. Despite the title, this is the will of John Jacob of Gosbeck, 1731.

Jancks

See Tettrell

Jessop

'Will of Elizabeth Jessop, 1718', *E.A.M.* **1929**, 87.

Judd

M., R.W. 'Will of Robert Judd of Brandon Ferry, 1681', *E.A.M.* **1918**, 69-70.

Keble

M., R.W. 'Will of Richard Keble of Old Newton, 1683', *E.A.M.* **1907**, 72.

Kederton

R[EDSTONE], V.B. 'Will of Richard Kederton, 1461', *E.A.M.* **1929**, 30-31. See also 33.

Keer

B., A. 'Will of Elizabeth Keer of Cretingham, 1787', *E.A.M.* **1922**, 36.

Kempe

B., A. 'Will of Edmond Kempe of Chediston, 1625', *E.A.M.* **1918**, 48-9 and 56.

Kew

B., A. 'Will of John Kew, of Brockford', *E.A.M.* **1921**, 15, 16 and 18.

Latham

W[AYMAN], H.W.B. 'Will of John Latham, clerk, of Westley, Co.Suffolk, 1717', *E.A.M.* **1911**, 10-11 and 13.

Lebbard

DULLEY, MORTON. 'Old wills: Walter Lebbard of Warlingham, 1514', *East Anglian* **3**, 1866-8, 81-2.

Legatt

'Old wills: Richard Legatt of Dennington, 1485', *East Anglian* **3**, 1866-8, 33-4.

Lucas

B., A. 'Will of Gibson Lucas, D.D., of Horringshearth, 1696', *E.A.M.* **1923**, 2.

Lyst

P[ARTRIDGE], C. 'Will of Richard Lyst of Bedingfield, 1630', *E.A.M.* **1932**, 2-3.

Makyn

BARTRUM, H.H. 'Will of William Makyn, 1473', *E.A.M.* **1909**, 108-9.

Mann

P[ARTRIDGE], C. 'Will of Edward Mann of Ipswich, 1680', *E.A.M.* **1928**, 14 and 16.

Marshe

DEEDES, CECIL. 'Will of Robert Marshe of Bromeswell', *East Anglian* N.S. **2**, 1887-8, 233-4. 1526.

Mason

A. 'Will of Rad Mason of Hartest, 1496', *E.A.M.* **1921**, 26.

M., R.W. 'Will of Humfry Mason of Aldborough, 1639', *E.A.M.* **1908**, 103.

May

S., F.H. 'The will of Thomas May, 1545', *E.A.M.* **1909**, 34.

Moore

L., H.R. 'Will of Francis Moore, 1734', *E.A.M.* **1928**, 12.

'Will of Walter Moore of Blakenham, 1522', *E.A.M.* **1907**, 49-50.

Mulliner

GRACE, FRANK. 'The administration of a late seventeenth century will', *Suffolk review* **12**, 1989, 18-25 and **13**, 1989, 6-11. Will of William Mulliner, 1698, with executor's accounts; inventory of Robert Mulliner, 1698.

Nayler

'Will of Thomas Nayler, 1757', *E.A.M.* **1928**, 18.

Neeche

F., E. 'Will of John Neeche, 1660', *E.A.M.* **1907**, 110.

Nunn

P[ARTRIDGE], C. 'Will of John Nunn of Sproughton, 1503', *E.A.M.* **1926**, 4-5 and 9-10.

Partridge

PARTRIDGE, CHARLES. 'Partridge of Acton, Sudbury, and Lavenham, Suffolk', *S.I.A.* **10**, 1900, 150-63. Wills; includes pedigree, 15th c. Not completed.

P[ARTRIDGE], C. 'Partridge wills, 1465 to 1477', *E.A.M.* **1925**, 81, 83, 84 and 86.

'Three Suffolk wills of the first half of the sixteenth century', *East Anglian* N.S. **11**, 1905-6, 273-7 and 311-12. Wills of Robert Partryche of Acton, 1525, George Pateriche of Lavenham, 1542 and Isbell Partrich of Acton, 1545.

'An Orford will, 1551', *E.A.M.* **1912**, 68. Will of Robert Parterydge.

PARTRIDGE, CHARLES. 'Will of Richard Partriche of Kersey and Bromeswell, 1610', *East Anglian* **10**, 1903-4, 281-3. Includes pedigree, 16-17th c.

'Will of Robert Parterich, 1656', *E.A.M.* **1912**, 103.

P[ARTRIDGE], C. 'Will of Richard Partridge, Capel S.Mary, 1670', *E.A.M.* **1927**, 56, 57-8, 60 and 64.

PARTRIDGE, CHARLES. 'A Suffolk yeoman's household goods, 1789', *Notes and queries* **192**, 1947, 447-50. See also 558-60. Inventory of Arthur Partridge.

PARTRIDGE, CHARLES. 'A Suffolk yeoman's household goods, 1794', *Notes and queries* **194**, 1949, 1-4. See also p.116-7 and 269-7. Inventory of Robert Partridge.

Pettus

L., H.R. 'Will of Lady Pettus, 1780', *E.A.M.* **1952**, 3-4.

Poly

'Will of John Poly of Fressingfield, 1590', *E.A.M.* **1934**, 11.

Potter

'The will of Thomas Potter of Chediston, 1633', *E.A.M.* **1908**, 44-5.

'Will of Thomas Potter, 1633', *E.A.M.* **1912**, 111 and 113-4.

Powrdy

B., A. 'Will of Edmund Powrdy of Botesdale, 1531', *E.A.M.* **1920**, 102-3, 107 and 109-10.

Pratt

W., H.W. 'Family of Pratt of East Anglia', *East Anglian* N.S. **7**, 1897-8, 294-5. Wills, mainly Suffolk.

Proctor

B., A. 'Will of Anne Proctor of Weybread, 1678', *E.A.M.* **1921**, 77, 79 and 81.

Punt

L., H.R. 'Bury widow's bequests, 1758', *E.A.M.* **1956**, 14 and 15. Will of Catherine Punt.

Pyerd

M., R.W. 'Will of Stephen Pyerd, 1602', *E.A.M.* **1910**, 20.

Pylbergh

B., H.W. 'A medieval yeoman's will', *East Anglian* N.S. **6**, 1895-6, 158-9. Will of William Pylbergh, 1500.

Quynton

HASLEWOOD, FRANCIS. 'The will of Sir Walter Quynton of Ipswich', *S.I.A.* **7**, 1891, 111-12. 1501.

Rawlins

'Will of John Rawlins of Fressingfield, clarke, 1629', *E.A.M.* **1934**, 17-18.

Reyff

'Will of Roger Reyff, of Melford, 1500', *E.A.M.* **1917**, 16-17.

Ruggle

'Will of George Ruggle, 1621', *E.A.M.* **1908**, 51.

Rye

BATES, T.H. 'Rhyming will of Robert Rye', *East Anglian* **3**, 1866-8, 247-8. 1550.

Schepper

'Will of Richard Schepper, 1458', *E.A.M.* **1934**, 27. Of Fressingfield.

Scruton

BALLENTYNE, MRS. [ed.] 'Transcript of the will of Alyce Scruton', *R. & B.* **2**(2), 1987, 10-11.

Searson

S., S. 'Will of Stephen Searson of Ipswich, 1771', *E.A.M.* **1926**, 16-17.

Seckford

B., A. 'Will of Mrs. Dorathy Sekeford, 1672', *E.A.M.* **1918**, 31, 36, 39 and 41-2.

Sherman

SMITH, CHAS. 'The will of Bezaleel Sherman, of St.Lawrence, Ipswich, grocer', *E.A.M.* **1910**, 1. 1617.

Probate Records *continued*

Sherman *continued*
'Wills of the Shermans of Yaxley in Suffolk',
*New England historical and genealogical
register* **54**, 1900, 62-9 and 152-62. 16-17th c.

Smith
B., A. 'Will of Elizabeth Smith of Monewdon,
1789', *E.A.M.* **1922**, 86.

O., J.R. 'Rattlesden wills', *East Anglian* N.S. **11**,
1905-6, 286-7. Wills of George Smith, 1559,
and William Harwell, 1578.

Stanton
'The will of Nicholas Stanton, minister of
St.Margaret's, Ipswich, 1649', *East Anglian*
N.S. **8**, 1899-1900, 193-5.

Steward
GREENING, S. 'Inventories', *Pagus* **15**, 1986, 14-16.
Includes inventory of Gyles Steward, 1705.

Stokys
SCHOMBERG, ARTHUR. 'Will of John Stokys, rector
of Gyslyngham, 1407', *M.G.H.* 3rd series **4**,
1902, 114. Gislingham.

Storar
'Will of William Storar alias Waren, 1558',
E.A.M. **1934**, 67-8.

Stubbin
PARTRIDGE, CHARLES. 'Extracts from the will of
Josiah Stubbin of Offton, 1686', *East Anglian*
N.S. **10**, 1903-4, 365-6.

Styward
MUNDAY, J.T. *Styward's substance.* Lakenheath
records, **5**. Lakenheath: the author, 1970. Will
of Simeon Styward, 1566.

Symonds
'Will of John Symonds of Cotton, 1674', *E.A.M.*
1914, 5.

Talbott
P[ARTRIDGE], C. 'Talbott of W.Suffolk', *E.A.M.*
1929, 76 and 77-8. 18th c., includes wills.

Temple
S., F.H. 'Will of Sir Alexander Temple', *E.A.M.*
1908, 58. See also **1909**, 11. 1629.

Tettrell
STATHAM, M.P. 'Nuncupative will of Jone Tettrell,
otherwise Jancks, of Acton, widow', *Suffolk
review* **1**, 1958, 192-3.

Thorne
'Will of the Rev. William Thorne, 1718', *E.A.M.*
1946, 19, 21 and 22-3.

Toller
'Old wills, no.III: William Toller of Downham,
Suffolk, 1503', *East Anglian* **1**, 1863, 403.

Toppesfield
F., E. 'Will of Anne Toppesfield, 1563', *E.A.M.*
1933, 85-6.

Trumpoor
'Will of Thomas Trumpoor alias Euston',
*Proceedings of the Bury and West Suffolk
Archaeological Institute* **1**, 1853, 267-8. 1440.

Tusser
CLARK, CHARLES, ed. *The last will and testament of
Thomas Tusser ... To which is added his
metrical autobiography, etc.* Great Totham: C.
Clark, 1846.

Tye
'Tye wills', *E.A.M.* **1907**, 31. Wills of Thomas
Tye, of South Elmham, 1510, and Thomas Tye,
of Framlingham, 1521.
'Will of Thomas Tye of Framlingham', *E.A.M.*
1907, 26-7. 1521.
'Will of John Tye, 1532', *E.A.M.* **1907**, 33.
'Will of Margery Tye, 1560', *E.A.M.* **1907**, 28-9.

Tylney
PARTRIDGE, CHARLES. 'Will of Sir Philip Tylney of
Shelley Hall, Suffolk', *Notes and queries* **192**,
1947, 297-300.

Unger
B., A. 'Will of John Unger of Woolpit, 1637',
E.A.M. **1916**, 79.

Waller
P[ARTRIDGE], C. 'Waller of Framlingham: will of
Thomas, 1560', *E.A.M.* **1929**, 12.
P[ARTRIDGE], C. 'Waller: will of Pheneas of
Dunwich, 1592', *E.A.M.* **1929**, 18.

Walpole
WALPOLE, J.E. 'Will of Sir Robert Walpole of
Westley, 1495', *E.A.M.* **1921**, 52 and 54-5.
WALPOLE, J.E. 'Will of Robert Walpole of Reydon,
1520', *E.A.M.* **1921**, 58.
WALPOLE, J.E. 'Will of William Walpole of
Halesworth, 1520', *E.A.M.* **1921**, 56.
WALPOLE, J.E. 'Will of Richard Waypull of
Heveningham, 1537', *E.A.M.* **1921**, 61.
WALPOLE, J.E. 'Will of William Wallpole of
Halesworth, 1539', *E.A.M.* **1921**, 62.
WALPOLE, JOHN. 'Will of Henry Walpull of South
Elmham, 1546', *E.A.M.* **1921**, 86-7.
WALPOLE, JOHN. 'Will of Nicholas Walpole of
Bramfield, 1557', *E.A.M.* **1921**, 93.

Walpole *continued*

WALPOLE, JOHN. 'Will of Robert Wapull of Raydon, near Southwold, 1559', *E.A.M.* **1921**, 83.

WALPOLE, JOHN. 'Will of John Walpole of Ipswich, 1567', *E.A.M.* **1921**, 88.

WALPOLE, JOHN. 'Will of Henry Walpole of Halesworth, 1568', *E.A.M.* **1921**, 90.

WALPOLE, JOHN. 'Will of Nicholas Walpole of Halesworth, 1569', *E.A.M.* **1921**, 95.

WALPOLE, JOHN. 'Will of John Walpole of Yoxford, 1597', *E.A.M.* **1922**, 3.

WALPOLE, JOHN. 'Will of Edward Wallpule of Rendham, 1635', *E.A.M.* **1922**, 31.

WALPOLE, JOHN. 'Will of John Walpoole of Beccles, 1663', *E.A.M.* **1922**, 29.

Walton

'Will of Henry Walton, 1813', *E.A.M.* **1909**, 2-3.

Ward

S., S. 'Will of Amy Ward of Mendham, 1639', *E.A.M.* **1926**, 20.

APPLEBY, JOHN S. 'Gooton man's goods and debts, 1688', *E.A.M.* **1950**, 17, 19, 21 and 22. Inventory of Thomas Ward, 1658.

Waren

See Storar

Warner

TYMMS, SAMUEL. 'Will of Sir Henry Warner, Knt., of Wamhill Hall, Mildenhall', *Proceedings of the Bury and West Suffolk Archaeological Institute* 1, 1853, 296-302. 1617.

Watkins

B., A. 'Will of John Watkins of Monowden, 1809', *E.A.M.* **1922**, 88 and 89.

Wayman

BLOOM, J. HARVEY. *Wayman wills and administrations preserved in the Prerogative Court of Canterbury, 1383-1821*. W. Gandy, 1922.

Webb

M., R.W. 'The will of Roger Webb of Cowling', *E.A.M.* **1911**, 77. Undated, ? 17th c.

Welch

'Will of Mary Welch, 1763', *E.A.M.* **1908**, 110.

Whatloke

'Will of George Whatloke of Clare, 1539', *Proceedings of the Bury and West Suffolk Archaeological Institute* 1, 1853, 186-90. See also 278-85.

Wheeler

S., S. 'Will of Susan Wheeler of Eye', *E.A.M.* **1926**, 15.

Whetcroft

MUSKETT, J.J. 'Suffolk wills from the Prerogative Court of Canterbury: Whetcroft of Suffolk', *S.I.A.* **6**, 1888, 94-104. Will of Henry Whetcroft, 1616, with pedigree, 16-17th c.

Wythipoll

MUSKETT, J.J. 'Wythipoll family of Ipswich. Wills of Edmund and Frances Wythipoll', *East Anglian* N.S. **10**, 1903-4, 85-9. Wills of Edmund, 1606, and Dame Frances, 1626.

Yates

'Will of Dr. John Yates, 1657', *E.A.M.* **1934**, 18-19.

Yong

'Inventory of Pastor Yong's estate', *E.A.M.* **1938**, 2. 1675.

11. OFFICIAL LISTS OF NAMES

Lists of names are invaluable sources of information for genealogists, especially when they cover the whole country and include everyone. Unfortunately the earliest such list was not compiled until the 1841 census and even then there are doubts as to whether everyone was included. However, many partial lists have been compiled, and some have been published. The earliest is Domesday Book, conveniently available in the Phillimore edition:

RUMBLE, ALEX, ed. *Domesday Book, 34: Suffolk.* 2 vols. Chichester: Phillimore, 1986.

Tax records

Between the 13th and the 17th centuries, various exactions were imposed upon the subjects of the crown—the poll tax, feudal aids, loans, ship money, etc. Some of the returns from these miscellaneous sources of revenue have been published; their importance for the genealogist is that they give names, and thus enable us to locate the people of the past in time and place. The following list is arranged chronologically.

POWELL, EDGAR. 'The taxation of Ipswich for the Welsh war in 1282', *S.I.A.* **12**, 1906, 137-57.

POWELL, EDGAR, ed. *A Suffolk hundred in the year 1283: the assessment of the Hundred of Blackbourne for a tax of one-thirtieth, and a return showing the land tenures there.* Cambridge: C.U.P., 1910.

MUNDAY, J.T. *A feudal aid roll for Suffolk, 1302-03.* Lakenheath: the author, 1973. Levied on knights fees.

PARTRIDGE, CHARLES. 'Suffolk surnames in 1340', *East Anglian* N.S. **5**, 1893-4, 225-9, 245-8, 259-61, 280-2 and 307-8. Extracts from the Nonarum Inquisitiones.

POWELL, EDGAR. *The rising in East Anglia in 1381, with an appendix containing the Suffolk Poll Tax lists for that year.* Cambridge: C.U.P., 1896.

POWELL, EDGAR. 'Transcripts of all the poll-tax lists which remain in the Record Office for the hundreds of Thingo and Lackford', *Royal Historical Society transactions* N.S. **8**, 1894, 227-49. For 1381.

POWELL, EDGAR. 'A Suffolk return for the three groat poll tax of 1381', *East Anglian* N.S. **5**, 1893-4, 369-70. Returns for an unknown Suffolk parish, with names of taxpayers.

Tax records *continued*

BULLEN, R. FREEMAN. 'The Spanish Armada and Suffolk, 1588', *E.A.M.* **1907**, 123-4 and 126-7. List of contributors towards the defence of the country.

M., J.J. 'A Suffolk directory: temp. James I', *East Anglian* N.S. **8**, 1899-1900, 289-95. List of Suffolk contributors to a loan, c.1612.

WAYMAN, H.W.B. 'The loans from Suffolk, 1627', *East Anglian* N.S. **13**, 1909-10, 6-7.

REDSTONE, VINCENT B., ed. *Ship-money returns for the county of Suffolk, 1639-40. (Harl. MSS. 7, 540-7, 542).* Ipswich: W.E. Harrison, 1904. Incomplete—returns for 80 parishes are missing—but lists many tax-payers.

WINN, ARTHUR T. *Aldeburgh Poll Tax, 1641.* Colchester: Benham & Co., 1926. Full transcript.

The most important levy from the 14th to the 17th century was the subsidy. The returns from this tax have survived in bulk, and those for Suffolk in 1327, 1524 and 1568 have been published in full. These effectively provide virtually complete lists of Suffolk heads of households. The following list of published subsidy returns is arranged chronologically.

Suffolk in 1327, being a subsidy return. S.G.B. **9**, vol.11. Woodbridge: George Booth, 1906.

'Suffolk Subsidy Roll 180/6: 1 Edward III, (1327): Hundred de Lacford', *East Anglian* N.S. **5**, 1893-4, 51-4, 87-90, 135-7 and 169-71.

H[ERVEY], S.H.A. *Suffolk in 1524, being the return for a subsidy granted in 1523.* S.G.B. **10**. Woodbridge: George Booth, 1910.

'A subsidy of 1552', *E.A.M.* **1930**, 7. List of subsidy commissioners.

H[ERVEY], S.H.A. *Suffolk in 1568, being the return for a subsidy granted in 1566.* S.G.B. **12**. Bury St.Edmunds: Paul & Mathew, 1909.

'Subsidy Roll: Suffolk, 8 Elizabeth', *East Anglian* N.S. **3**, 1889-90, 241-4. For the Hundred of Lackford, and also for Hawstead. Names.

POWELL, EDGAR. 'Subsidy Roll, Suffolk: 15 Car I, Hundred of Lackford and Half Hundred of Exning', *East Anglian* N.S. **4**, 1891-2, 170-71.

Muster rolls

Muster rolls offer another potential source of information. All adult males were obliged to bear arms for the defence of the realm, and to appear at musters, where their names were entered on a roll. A number of these rolls have been published:

BEDELL, A.J. 'Unpublished muster-roll of the reign of Richard I: Norfolk and Suffolk', *East Anglian* N.S. **4**, 1891-2, 225-9.

POUND, JOHN, ed. *The military survey of 1522 for Babergh Hundred*. S.R.S., **28**. Woodbridge: Boydell Press, 1986. The survey was intended "to obtain reasonably accurate details of individual wealth as a prelude to the levying of subsidies", and is almost a full list of heads of households.

'Edwardstone: its church and priory', *S.I.A.* **15**, 1915, 87-99. Includes 1522 muster roll, with list of vicars and patrons, 1556-1806.

POWELL, EDGAR. 'Muster rolls of the territorials in Tudor times', *S.I.A.* **15**, 1915, 113-43 and 238-52; **16**, 1918, 36-43, 90-97 and 211-18; **18**, 1924, 180-210, and **19**, 1927, 52-71 and 212-26. Includes rolls for various hundreds, 1534-84.

REDSTONE, V.B. 'Muster roll of Babergh Hundred, 1577, 1579', *E.A.M.* **1937**, passim. List by parish.

WAYMAN, H.W. BILLING. 'Muster-roll of two hundred footmen from the Hundreds of Hoxon and Plomesgate under Sir Thomas Glenham, Knight, A.D.1631', *East Anglian* N.S. **13**, 1909-10, 132-5, 150-51 and 163-4.

BANKS, CHARLES EDWARD, ed. *Able men of Suffolk, 1638: transcribed from the original in the Public Record Office ... state papers domestic Charles I, vol.411*. Boston, Mass.: Anglo-American Records Foundation, 1931.

R[EDSTONE], V.B. 'Parliamentary supporters at Lavenham', *E.A.M.* **1937**, 4, 5, 7 and 9. List of volunteers supplying arms, 1640s.

Loyalty oaths

The question of allegiance was the major issue of the Civil War. To whom was loyalty due—King, or Parliament? Oaths of loyalty were demanded from the populace at various times, and were recorded for posterity by signatures. The Protestation returns of 1641/2 give the signatures of almost all adult males. For Suffolk, the returns from two parishes are in print:

'Leiston folk in 1641', *E.A.M.* **1931**, 14-15.

CROUCH, CHARLES HALL. 'The Wanstead protestation, 1641', *E.A.M.* **1922**, 81. Found in the parish register.

See also:

MORLEY, CLAUDE. 'Solumne League and Covenant in Suffolk', *E.A.M.* **1945**, 30, 32, 33-4 and 35. See also 36. List of those who signed the covenant, 1643.

RAVEN, JOHN JAMES. 'List of subscriptions to the engagement of 1651', *New England historical and genealogical register* **44**, 1890, 365-6. Signatures from Dennington, Suffolk.

Hearth Tax

The restoration of Charles II in 1660 did not mean the end of Stuart financial exactions. Rather, the years which followed witnessed a search for new sources of government finance. One result was the hearth tax. This did not result in a bonanza for the government—but it did for the genealogist. The hearth tax returns provide a fairly complete list of Suffolk heads of households in 1674, which every genealogist should consult:

H[ERVEY], S.H.A., ed. *Suffolk in 1674, being the hearth tax returns*. S.G.B. **11**(13). Woodbridge: George Booth, 1905.

See also:

GREENING, SYLVIA. 'The hearth tax', *Pagus* **5**, 1984, 2-5. Transcript for Barrow.

COLMAN, SYLVIA. 'The hearth tax returns for the Hundred of Blackbourne, 1662', *S.I.A.* **32**, 1973, 168-92.

Defence contributors

Contributors to the defence of the realm against the 1745 rebellion are listed in:

BULLEN, R. FREEMAN. 'Suffolk and the 'forty-five', *E.A.M.* **1910**, 66-7, 69, 72, 75, 77-8 and 133-4.

Poll books

During the 18th and 19th centuries, Parliamentary elections were not secret, and many poll books listing electors and how they cast their votes were published. Both printed and manuscript pollbooks are identified in the companion volume to the present work, *English genealogy: an introductory bibliography*. Reference may also be made to Steward's *Bibliography of Suffolk,* (see above, 9) and to:

'Suffolk Poll books', *East Anglian* N.S. **4**, 1891-2, 383; N.S. **5**, 1893-4, 14-15 and 143.

BULLEN, R. FREEMAN. 'Suffolk poll books', *Notes and queries* 11th Series **1**, 1910, 306.

Census

Much the most useful official lists, for the genealogist, are those deriving from the nineteenth century censuses. For Suffolk, many brief extracts, etc., from the enumerators returns have been published; they are listed here by date and place.

Official Lists of Names *continued*

General

PERKINS, NORMAN. 'Census returns: Westerfield, near Ipswich', *S.Rt.* **9**(3), 1983, 59-61; **9**(4), 1983, 84-5. Lists surnames, 1841-81, indicating no. of occurences in each decade.

1841

'Back to the hulks', *S.Rt.* **16**(1), 1990, 46-9. Suffolk convicts held on prison hulks in 1841.

1851

SUFFOLK FAMILY HISTORY SOCIETY. *Suffolk 1851 census index.* 8 vols. in 25 pts. Colchester: the Society, 1989-91. Contents: v.1: South West Suffolk; v.2: South Suffolk; v.3: S.W. Suffolk (Sudbury Dist.); v.4: Central-South Suffolk (Cosford Dist.); v.5: Central-West Suffolk (Thingoe Dist.); v.6: Bury St.Edmunds; v.7: North-West Suffolk (Mildenhall Dist.); v.8: Central-North Suffolk (Stow Dist.).

Hargrave

SLADE, MARGARET. '1851 census return for Hargrave', *Pagus* **21**, 1987, 12-29. Full transcript.

Rushmere

KIGHTLEY, D. 'Census returns, 1851: Rushmere St.Andrew, near Ipswich, Suffolk', *S.Rt.* **8**(4), 71. Surnames only.

DANIEL, R.A. 'Was your missing person in a prison hulk?', *S.Rt.* **15**(4), 1989, 187-9. Suffolk entries from 1851 census return from various hulks at Portsmouth, Gosport, Woolwich, Bermuda and Gibraltar.

Hull and Kensington

EDMONDS, JENNIFER A. *Born in Norfolk or Suffolk: a collection of 1851 census strays from Kensington and Hull.* [The author], [1989].

Parkhurst

HERRIDGE, K. '1851 census, Parkhurst barracks, Newport I.O.W., (part of HO107/1663)', *S.Rt.* **15**(4), 1989, 175. Lists Suffolk soldiers.

1861

Parkhurst Barracks

HERRIDGE, KEVIN. 'Parkhurst Barracks, Newport, Isle of Wight, 1861 census, RG9/655', *S.Rt.* **14**(4), 1988, 110.

1871

Horfield, Gloucestershire

'Suffolk-born orphans 1871 census, Horfield parish', *S.Rt.* **17**(1), 1991, 12-13. From Horfield, Gloucestershire.

Middlesborough, Yorkshire

CHILVERS, T. 'East Anglian immigrants to Teeside in the 1860's', *S.Rt.* **3**(3), 1977, 89-90; **3**(4), 1977, 104-5; **4**(1), 1978, 6; **4**(2), 1978, 27; **4**(3), 1978, 37; **5**(1), 1979, 12-13. Extracts from 1871 Middlesborough census.

Rushmere St.Andrew

KIGHTLEY, DAVID. '1871 census: Rushmere St.Andrew (nr. Ipswich, Suffolk)', *S.Rt.* **7**(3), 1981, 53. Lists surnames only.

1881

The Mormons are currently preparing a microfishe index to the 1881 census. This will be an essential tool for every genealogist. See also:

Barrow

GREENING, S. '1881 census', *Pagus* **25**, 1988, 8-18. For Barrow.

Ipswich

'List of prisoners in Her Majesty's prison, Ipswich, 1881', *S.Rt.* **17**(1), 1991, 60-61. From the census.

New Windsor, Berkshire

CULLINGHAM, GORDON. 'Strays: 1881 census of New Windsor: extracts of persons from Suffolk/Norfolk', *S.Rt.* **8**(4), 1982, 78-9; **9**(1), 1983, 9-10; **9**(2), 37-9.

Sudbury

MURRELLS, D.J. 'An index covering names occurring in the 1881 census of Sudbury, Suffolk', *S.Rt.* **15**(5), 1990, 233-9.

Woolwich Barracks, Kent

'1881 census (RG10775-778) for Woolwich Barracks, Kent: extracts of soldiers born in Suffolk', *S.Rt.* **14**(3), 1988, 82.

Landowners

A different census was taken in 1873: everyone who owned an acre or more of land was listed, and the returns for Suffolk are printed in:

Return of owners of land, 1873: Suffolk. House of Commons papers, 1874, **72**(2), 341-85.

12. DIRECTORIES AND MAPS

Directories provide invaluable listings of former inhabitants; for the nineteenth century, they are the equivalent of the modern phone book. I have endeavoured to identify all those relating to Suffolk published in the nineteenth century; selected directories for the twentieth century are also included in the following list, which is arranged chronologically and by place.

Directories covering a large number of counties are not included here; they may be identified by consulting the sources listed in the companion to the present work, *English genealogy: an introductory bibliography*.

Pigot and Co's national commercial directory, comprising a directory and classification of the merchants, bankers, professional gentlemen, manufacturers and traders in ... Norfolk & Suffolk. J. Pigot and Co., 1830. Reprinted King's Lynn: Michael Winton, 1992.

WHITE, WILLIAM. *History, gazetteer and directory of Suffolk and the towns near its borders ...* Sheffield: R. Leader, 1844-92. 6 issues. 1844 issue reprinted Newton Abbot: David & Charles, 1970.

Slater's (late Pigot & Co.) Royal national and commercial directory of the counties of Bedfordshire, Cambridgeshire, Huntingdonshire, Lincolnshire, Norfolk, Northampton and Suffolk ... Manchester: Isaac Slater, 1850.

Kelly's directory of Suffolk. W. Kelly & Co., 1853-1937. 20 issues; title varies. Sometimes referred to as *Post Office directory ...* and issued at different times in one volume with various other counties.

J.G. Harrod and Co's postal and commercial directory of Suffolk ... Thomas Danks, 1864-77. 3 issues; the 1873 and 1877 editions also include Cambridgeshire.

Morris & Co's commercial directory and gazetteer of Suffolk with Great Yarmouth and Newmarket. Nottingham: Morris & Co., 1868. Great Yarmouth, Norfolk, Newmarket, partially Cambridgeshire.

GLYDE, JOHN. *Glyde's Suffolk almanac annual and official directory for 18-- .* Smart & Allen, 1880-90. Annual. No lists of inhabitants, but some issues do include a 'Who's Who' of Suffolk, plus lists of clergy, etc.

Deacon's Cambridgeshire, Norfolk and Suffolk court guide and county blue book: a fashionable record, professional register, and general survey of the counties ... Charles William Deacon & Co., 1886-93.

Suffolk county handbook and official directory ... with which are incorporated Knights' county handbook and Glyde's Suffolk almanack, with map of the county. Ipswich: Ipswich Journal Printing & Publishing Co., 1896-1939.

Beccles

Arthur Stebbings' directory to Beccles ... Lowestoft: Arthur Stebbings, 1886.

Brandeston

BRANDESTON HALL HISTORY SOCIETY. *Survey of the parish of Brandeston.* Woodbridge: the Society, 1971. Effectively a directory for 1971, with some historical information.

Felixstowe

Directory of Felixstowe, Walton, and Trimley. Felixstowe: W.S. Cowell, 1924-34. 3 issues.

Ipswich

Directory of Ipswich and neighbourhood, with Felixstowe, Walton, Hadleigh, Needham Market, Stowmarket and Woodbridge, etc. Geo. Stevens, 1881-94. 3 issues; title varies.

Directory of Ipswich, together with Felixstowe, Walton, Harwich, Dovercourt, and villages adjoining Ipswich. Ipswich: Jarrold & Sons, 1890.

Jewell's Ipswich directory, together with Felixstowe, Hadleigh, Stowmarket, Walton, Woodbridge and other adjoining parishes. Ipswich: G.W. Jewell, 1898.

Kelly's directory of Ipswich ... Kelly's, 1899-1949. Annual except for war years.

Halesworth

Arthur Stebbings' directory to Halesworth ... Lowestoft: Arthur Stebbings, 1886.

Lowestoft

Kelly's directory of Lowestoft and Kirkley, with Beccles and neighbourhood ... Kelly's Directories, 1899-1949. Almost annual.

LEES, HUGH D.W. 'Some notes on Lees' survey of Lowestoft', *Genealogists magazine* **16**, 1969-71, 159-61. Description of project recording 'who lived where' in Lowestoft.

Mathieson's Yarmouth and Lowestoft directory for 1867-68. Lowestoft: Samuel Tymms, 1867. N.B. Great Yarmouth is in Norfolk.

Woodbridge

Read's illustrated family almanack and Woodbridge directory for 1888. [Woodbridge]: Read, 1888.

Maps

In addition to directories, the genealogist also needs maps—and especially historic maps—to identify the places mentioned in his sources. Of particular value are the first edition 1" Ordnance Survey maps; these were made accurately, at a date before the landscape became afflicted with the concrete jungle of modern suburbia. A convenient modern edition is provided by:

The Old Series Ordnance Survey maps of England and Wales, scale: 1 inch to 1 mile: a reproduction of the 110 sheets of the survey in early state in 10 volumes. Volume 1: Kent, Essex, E. Sussex, and S. Suffolk. Volume 5: Lincolnshire, Rutland and East Anglia. Lympne Castle: Harry Margary, 1975-87.

Reprinted sheet maps from the Ordnance Survey have also been published by David & Charles. An older map of the county has been reproduced by:

DYMOND, D.P., ed. *The county of Suffolk, surveyed by Joseph Hodskinson ... 1783.* S.R.S., **15**, 1972.

Many manuscript maps of Suffolk, 1580-1800, are listed in the Suffolk Record Office's *Archive news* **5, 7, 9, 11, 12** and **17**, 1975-81, passim.

Reference must also be made to the map of Suffolk parish boundaries published by the Institute of Heraldic and Genealogical Studies. This should be in the possession of every Suffolk genealogist.

A general and most useful atlas of the county is provided by:

DYMOND, DAVID & MARTIN, EDWARD, eds. *An historical atlas of Suffolk.* 2nd ed. Ipswich: Suffolk County Council, 1989. This includes many maps depicting, e.g. Roman Catholic recusancy, education before 1750, population trends 1811-1981, etc., together with many bibliographical notes.

13. RELIGIOUS RECORDS

The involvement of the church in everyday life was formerly much wider than it is today, and its records are of the greatest importance to genealogists. Some of these records, i.e. parish registers, probate records, and churchwardens accounts, are dealt with in other chapters of this book. This chapter focuses on more explicitly ecclesiastical records which record the names of clergy, churchwardens and others involved in the work of the church. The first section is devoted to general works, and is arranged in rough chronological order:

MORLEY, CLAUDE. 'Catalogue of beneficed clergy of Suffolk, 1086-1550', *S.I.A.* **22**,1934, 29-85.

LANDON, L. 'Early archdeacons of Norwich diocese', *S.I.A.* **20**, 1930, 11-35. List, 11-13th c., Norfolk and Suffolk.

'Early Suffolk rectors', *E.A.M.* **1908**, 78 and 79-80. List from 13th c. papal registers.

LE NEVE, JOHN. *Fasti ecclesiae Anglicanae, 1300-1541. IV: monastic cathedrals (Southern Province),* comp. B. Jones. Athlone Press, 1963. Includes lists of the Archdeacons of Sudbury and Suffolk.

'Excommunicated parsons, c.1390-1410', *E.A.M.* **1931**, 1-2. See also 7-8.

MANNING, R.C. 'First fruits, diocese of Norwich, temp. Henry VI and Edward IV: transcript of the account rolls of John de Lopham, collector of first fruits ... for the archdeaconries of Suffolk and Sudbury, temp. Henvy VI and Edward IV', *S.I.A.* **7**, 1891, 91-110. Lists clergy newly instituted.

JESSOPP, A., ed. *Visitations of the Diocese of Norwich, A.D.1492-1532.* Camden Society, N.S. **43**, 1888. Record of ecclesiastical visitations in Suffolk and Norfolk; gives many names of religious.

COZENS-HARDY, B., ed. *Norwich Consistory Court depositions, 1499-1512 and 1518-30.* Norfolk Record Society, **10**, 1938. Includes many Suffolk cases.

LINNELL, CHARLES LAWRENCE SCRUTON. *Some East Anglian clergy.* London: Fath P.; New York: Morehouse-Barlow, 1961. General discussion, 16-19th c.

PEARSON, W.C. 'Archdeaconry of Suffolk: mandates for induction, 1526-1629', *East Anglian* N.S. **6**, 1895-6, 75-6, 118-21, 173-5, 191-2, 247-50, 358-62 and 381-3; N.S. **8**, 1899-1900, 5-7, 27-9, 60-2, 72-4, 120-22, 147-9, 165-7, 181-3, 262-5, 278-81, 307-9 and 362-4; N.S. **9**, 1901-02, 28-30, 80-1 and 108-10.

BULLEN, R. FREEMAN. 'Catalogue of beneficed clergy of Suffolk, 1551-1631 (with a few of earlier date)', *S.I.A.* **22**,1936, 294-333.

GREEN, ABISHAI JAMES. *The Suffolk martyrs ... from Fox's book of martyrs*. Sudbury: George Williams Fulcher, 1851. Notes on 34 protestant martyrs.

HARPER, A.C. 'The martyrs of Suffolk under Queen Mary, 1553-1558', *S.Rt.* **3**(2), 1977, 72-3. Lists 32 protestant martyrs, with brief biographical notes.

BASKERVILLE, G. 'Married clergy and pensioned religious in Norwich diocese, 1555', *English Historical Review* **48**, 1933, 43-64 and 199-228. Gives many names of clergy in Norfolk and Suffolk.

BARTON, THOMAS F., ed. *The registrum vagum of Anthony Harison*. 2 vols. Norfolk Record Society, **32-3**, 1963-4. Includes list of the diocesan clergy, 1605, of ordinands and institutions, of excommunicants, recusants, clergy muster roll, 1608, and many other records of diocesan administration.

R[EDSTONE], V.B. 'A noate of arms, 1612', *E.A.M.* **1912**, 38-9, 40-41 and 43. List of clergy liable to provide arms at musters.

WILLIAMS, J.F., ed. *Diocese of Norwich: Bishop Redman's visitation, 1597: presentments in the archdeaconries of Norwich, Norfolk and Suffolk*. Norfolk Record Society, **18**, 1946. Includes presentments from the Archdeaconry of Suffolk. Gives names of many clergy, churchwardens, etc.

'The condition of the Archdeaconries of Suffolk and Sudbury in 1603', *S.I.A.* **6**, 1888, 361-400 and **11**, 1903, 1-46. Returns made to Archbishop Whitgift, including the names of all clergy, etc.

CARTER, E.H. *Norwich Subscription Books: a study of the subscription books of the Diocese of Norwich, 1637-1800*. Thomas Nelson & Sons, 1937. Lists clergy, schoolmasters, etc., who took the oath of faith.

BULLEN, R. FREEMAN. 'Sequestrations in Suffolk', *S.I.A.* **19**, 1927, 15-51 & 141-67. See also **24**, 1949, 125-7. Biographical dictionary of clergy ejected by Parliament in the 1640s.

HASLEWOOD, FRANCIS. 'Ministers of Suffolk ejected 1643-4', *S.I.A.* **9**, 1897, 307-9. List.

BULLEN, R. FREEMAN. 'The church in Suffolk under the Commonwealth, 1645-47', *E.A.M.* **1911**, 1-2, 3-4, 6-7, 8-9, 12, 15, 17, 21 and 23-4.

GRIGSON, FRANCIS. 'East Anglia institutions to benefices: no.4: Suffolk', *East Anglian* N.S. **1**, 1885-6, 105-7. By the Archbishop of Canterbury, 1660-1838.

Many works—mainly brief notes—provide lists of Church of England clergy, etc., and other information on the work of the church in particular places. They are listed here by parish.

Alpheton

BARTRUM, H.H. 'Rectors of Alpheton, Suffolk', *E.A.M.* **1909**, 2, 3, 5-6 and 10.

Ampton

WICKHAM, W.A. 'The parsons and patrons of Ampton', *S.I.A.* **18**, 1924, 123-43.

Bacton

HEMSWORTH, A.B. 'Bacton church', *S.I.A.* **5**, 1886, 186-94. Includes list of rectors.

Barking

L., H.R. 'Rectors of Barking, Suffolk', *E.A.M.* **1955**, passim. Lists with biographical notes.

Barnardiston

W., L.H.H. 'Barnardiston: list of rectors', *E.A.M.* **1932**, 26. 16-20th c.

Barton Mills

POWELL, EDGAR. 'List of rectors with sundry documents relating to church matters at Barton Mills', *S.I.A.* **13**, 1909, 178-90.

Brettenham

BETHAM, CHARLES JEPSON. 'Rectors of Brettenham', *S.I.A.* **8**, 1894, 117. 1308-1708.

Bury St.Edmunds

CULLUM, G. MILNER-GIBSON. 'Wednesday lecturers at St.James' church, Bury St.Edmunds, A.D.1685', *East Anglian* N.S. **3**, 1889-90, 188-9. List of ministers who delivered 'lectures', i.e. sermons.

THOMSON, RODNEY M. 'Obedientiaries of St.Edmunds Abbey', *S.I.A.* **35**, 1985, 91-103. Lists some 300 officers of the abbey at Bury St.Edmunds.

Butley

MYRES, J.N.L. 'Butley Priory, Suffolk', *Archaeological journal* **90**, 1933, 177-281. Includes list of priors and canons, list of 26 wills mentioning the Priory, and detailed abstracts of the wills of William Pakeman, 1504, and Henry Baret, 1516/17.

Religious Records *continued*

Cheveley
BENNETT, E.K. 'Cheveley church', *Proceedings of the Bury and West Suffolk Archaeological Institute* 1, 1853, 237-49. Includes list of clergy, and will extracts relating to pious bequests.

Dennington
'Rectors of Dennington', *S.I.A.* 8, 1894, 80-82. With brief biographical notes.

Freckenham
'St. Andrew's, Freckenham, Suffolk: list of rectors and vicars', *East Anglian* N.S. 13, 1909-10, 71-4.

Gisleham
B., E.R. 'Rectors of Gisleham', *E.A.M.* 1927, 73-4 and 75.

Great Waldingfield
HASLEWOOD, FRANCIS. 'Rectors of Great Waldingfield', *S.I.A.* 9, 1897, 94-101. List with biographical notes.

Hadleigh Deanery
'Hadleigh Deanery and its court', *S.I.A.* 15, 1915, 16-44. An edition of two act books, 1637-41 and 1668-70, including many names; amongst other matters, the court dealt with probate business.

Hawstead
MERCER, LESLIE. 'Rectors of Hawstead', *S.I.A.* 7, 1891, 334-6.

Hemingstone
L., W.M. 'Rectors of Hemingstone (St.Gregory)', *E.A.M.* 1931, 66 and 69. 1539-1885.

Hepworth
METHOLD, THOMAS TINDAL. 'The parish of Hepworth and its rectors', *S.I.A.* 8, 1894, 380-407. See also 18, 1924, 66-9. Includes biographical notes.

Ipswich
HASLEWOOD, FRANCIS. 'Saint Matthew's church, Ipswich', *S.I.A.* 7, 1891, 129-208. Includes list of rectors, with detailed biographical notes and some pedigrees, etc., also monumental inscriptions and parishioners wills, etc.
'Confirmed in 1636', *E.A.M.* 1931, 9. List of confirmees, St.Margarets, Ipswich.

Little Glemham
P[ARTRIDGE], C. 'Confirmed in 1636', *E.A.M.* 1931, 79-80. Confirmees at Little Glemham.

Martlesham
LINGWOOD, HAROLD R. 'The rectors of Martlesham', *S.I.A.* 25, 1952, 193-201. Includes detailed biographical notes.

Little Waldingfield
HASLEWOOD, FRANCIS. 'Vicars of Little Waldingfield', *S.I.A.* 9, 1897, 116-21. List with biographical notes.

Mettingham
MANNING, C.R. 'Extracts from the ancient accounts of Mettingham College, Suffolk', *Archaeological journal* 6, 1849, 62-8. Includes many 14th c. names.

Norton
'Rectors of Norton, Suffolk', *E.A.M.* 1913, 67-8 and 76-7.

Pakenham
JONES, CHARLES WILLIAM. 'The vicars of Pakenham', *S.I.A.* 8, 1894, 408-12.

Shelley
P[ARTRIDGE], C. 'Shelley: parishioners, 1663 to 1751', *E.A.M.* 1930, 51. Lists incumbents and churchwardens.

Shimpling
W., L.H.H. 'Shimpling registers', *E.A.M.* 1932, 55. List of rectors, 1620-1773.

Sibton
HASLEWOOD, FRANCIS. 'Vicars of Sibton', *S.I.A.* 8, 1894, 63. With brief biographical notes.

Stansfield
LITTLE, J.R. 'Stansfield parish notes', *S.I.A.* 10, 1900, 345-59. Includes list of rectors, etc.

Thedwastre Deanery
GRANSDEN, ANTONIA. 'Some late thirteenth-century records of an ecclesiastical court in the Archdeaconry of Sudbury', *Bulletin of the Institute of Historical Research* 32, 1959, 62-9. Gives names of those presented from the Deanery of Thedwastre.

Ufford
BULLEN, R. FREEMAN. 'Rectors of Ufford', *E.A.M.* 1921, 12. 1558-1903.

Walberswick
St. Andrew, Walberswick: history of the church and list of vicars back to A.D.1310. 9th ed. Southwold: A.D. Thompson, 1959.

Religious Records *continued*

Westerfield

PEARSON, WILLIAM C. 'Lists of confirmation candidates, 1636-1763: parish of Westerfield, Co.Suffolk', *East Anglian* N.S. **5**, 1893-4, 29-30.

Woodbridge

REDSTONE, VINCENT BURROUGH. 'The rectors and curates of Woodbridge', *S.I.A.* **9**, 1897, 354-8.

Wortham

F., F. 'The rectories and rectors of Wortham', *E.A.M.* **1920**, 41-2, 46, 48, 53, 55 and 58.

Nonconformists

Nonconformists in Suffolk are dealt with in a number of works:

RYE, WALTER. 'Popish and sectary recusants in Suffolk, 1596', *East Anglian* **2**, 1864-6, 159-60, 176-85. Lists both.

REDSTONE, V.B. *Records of protestant dissenters in Suffolk*. Woodbridge: George Booth, 1912. Lists meeting houses, with many names; also includes list of nonconformist registers then at Somerset House (now at the Public Record Office).

HOLMES, CLIVE, ed. *The Suffolk Committees for Scandalous Ministers, 1644-1646*. S.R.S., **13**, 1970. Records names of many clergy whose abilities and/or loyalties were questioned by the Parliamentary authorities.

JEWSON, C.B. 'Return of conventicles in Norwich diocese, 1669: Lambeth MS. no.639', *Norfolk Archaeology* **33**, 1965, 6-34. Gives many names of Suffolk and Norfolk nonconformists.

BULLEN, R.F. 'Nonconformist meeting places in Suffolk in 1672', *E.A.M.* **1920**, 42, 43-4, 46, 58, 61-2, 67-8 and 69-70. See also 52 and 64. Lists owners of meeting houses.

Baptists

KLAIBER, ASHLEY J. *The story of the Suffolk Baptists*. Kingsgate press, [c.1929?]. Includes some names.

PEDERSEN, MRS. 'Baptist Meeting House, Grundisburgh, Suffolk', *S.Rt.* **9**(1), 1983, 8. Index of surnames, presumably from church records; undated.

Congregationalists

BROWNE, JOHN. *History of Congregationalism and memorials of the churches in Norfolk and Suffolk*. Jarrold & Sons, 1877. Includes various lists of ministers, etc.

Congregationalists *continued*

HOSKEN, T.J. *History of Congregationalism and memorials of the churches of our order in Suffolk*. Ipswich: W.E. Harrison, 1920. Includes various lists of ministers, etc.

SYDENHAM, G. 'Source material for the history of Suffolk Congregationalism', *Suffolk review* **4**(2), 1973, 41-52. List of published and unpublished histories.

B[ULLEN], R.F. 'Notes on Congregational church, Bury St.Edmunds', *E.A.M.* **1925**, passim. Extracts from registers, list of members, etc., 17-18th c.

Independents

RIX, S.W. *Brief records of the Independent church at Beccles, Suffolk, including biographical notices of its ministers* ... Jackson & Walford, 1837.

R[EDSTONE], V.B. 'Independents of Bury St.Edmunds', *E.A.M.* **1940**, 37, 39 and 41; **1941**, 3, 6 and 7. Extracts from 17-18th c. minute books, giving members names.

PARSONS, K.A.C., ed. *The church book of the Independent Church (now Pound Lane Baptist) Isleham, 1693-1805*. Cambridge Antiquarian Records Society, **6**. 1984. Isleham is in Cambridgeshire, but many members of the church were from Suffolk.

Presbyterians

REDSTONE, V.B. 'Presbyterian church government in Suffolk, 1643-47', *S.I.A.* **13**, 1909, 133-75. Primarily extracts from the proceedings of the Parliamentary Committee for Plundered Ministers, giving much information on the clergy.

Quakers

FITCH, STANLEY H.G., ed. *Sudbury Quakers, 1655-1953: Extracts from various sources*. Bury St.Edmunds: West Suffolk Newpapers, [1954]. Includes many names.

MIZON, LIONEL. *Quakers of Haverhill, 1656-1873*. Haverhill: Haverhill and District Local History Group/Religious Society of Friends, 1984. Includes names of 'sufferers', 18-19th c., and list of births, marriages and deaths, 1768-1855.

Roman Catholics

M., R.W. 'Papists in East Anglia in 1585', *E.A.M.* **1911**, 17-18. List.

SMITH, CHAS. 'Popish recusants in Suffolk', *E.A.M.* **1911**, 50-51. See also 58. List, c.1665-85.

'Popish recusants in Suffolk', *East Anglian* N.S. **1**, 1885-6, 345-6. List, late 17th c.

Roman Catholics *continued*

C., J.L. 'Refusal of Roman Catholics to take the oath of allegiance', *East Anglian* N.S. **7**, 1897-8, 285-8. List of those fined in 1745, in Cambridgeshire, Suffolk, Essex and Norfolk.

ROWE, JOY. *The story of Catholic Bury St.Edmunds*. [Bury St.Edmunds?]: the author, 1980. Includes 156 names from Catholic registers, 1759-90.

Various lists of Suffolk sixteenth-century recusants are to be found in the *Publications of the Catholic Record Society* **18**, 1916, 309-25; **53**, 1961, 108-11; **57**, 1965, 157-70; and **61**, 1970, 88-95 and 223-8.

14. ESTATE AND FAMILY PAPERS

The records of estate administration constitute a mine of information for the genealogist. Much is in print, although far more lies untouched in the archives. A number of substantial editions of Suffolk deed abstracts are available:

RYE, WALTER. *A Calendar of the feet of fines for Suffolk*. Ipswich: W.E. Harrison for Suffolk Institute of Archaeology, 1900. 1189-1485.

DODWELL, BARBARA, ed. *Feet of fines for the county of Norfolk for the reign of King John, 1201-1215, for the county of Suffolk for the reign of King John, 1199-1214*. Pipe Roll Society publications, **70**, 1958.

For fines, see also:

RYE, WALTER. 'Some stray notes from Suffolk fines', *East Anglian* N.S. **1**, 1885-6, 65-6.

'A descriptive catalogue of ancient deeds in the Public Record Office', *S.I.A.* **10**, 1900, 251-344 and 399-413.

'The value of old parchment deeds in genealogical and topographical research', *Topographical quarterly* **3**(4), 1935, 269-306. One of a series of works giving numerous abstracts of deeds.

'List of deeds recently acquired by the Institute', *S.I.A.* 1930, 73-9. Listed by parish.

HALL, T. WALTER & THOMAS, A. HERMANN. *Descriptive catalogue of the charters, rolls, deeds, pedigrees, pamphlets, newspapers, monumental inscriptions, maps, and miscellaneous papers forming the Jackson Collection at the Sheffield Public Libraries*. Sheffield: J.W. Northend, 1914. Lists many Suffolk deeds, etc., as well as documents relating to Yorkshire, Derbyshire, Nottinghamshire and various other counties.

'Suffolk marriage settlements', *E.A.M.* **1930**, 57, 59-60, 61, 63 and 80; **1931**, 2, 4 and 7. Abstracts of 37 deeds.

OWEN, A.E.B. 'A scrivener's notebook from Bury St.Edmunds', *Archives* **14**(61), 1979, 16-21. Discussion of a notebook containing drafts of some 800 conveyances of the 1460s.

Manorial court rolls are another important source of information. Those held at the British Library (formerly the British Museum) for Suffolk, Norfolk, Essex and Cambridgeshire are listed in:

STEDMAN, A.E. 'East Anglian manor court rolls: mss. Department of the British Museum', *East Anglian* N.S. **13**, 1909-10, 22-4.

Enclosure awards frequently provide comprehensive lists of land owners and tenants at the date of the award. Those for Suffolk are listed in:

TATE, W.E. 'A handlist of Suffolk enclosure and awards', *S.I.A.* **25**, 1952, 225-63.
See also:
'Suffolk enclosure awards and maps', *Suffolk review* 2(6), 1963, 188-93.
An index of fee farm rents is provided by:
B[IDEN], L.M. 'Index to the particulars of fee-farm rents reserved upon grants from the Crown and remaining in the Augmentation Office: Suffolk', *East Anglian* N.S. **10**, 1903-4, 249-53, 274-6, 286-9 and 305-7.
The larger estate owners of Suffolk had lands in many parts of the county, and sometimes in other counties as well. The estate papers of a number of large proprietors have been listed and published:
Papers of Sir Nicholas Bacon in the University of Chicago Library. Special series, 25. List and Index Society, 1989.
TAYLOR, F. 'Hand-list of the Crutchley manuscripts in the John Rylands Library', *Bulletin of the John Rylands Library* 33(1), 1950, 138-87 and 327-72. Estate papers of the Coke family relating primarily to Derbyshire, Lancashire and Suffolk.
RIGG, J.M. 'Ancient deeds belonging to the Duke of Norfolk, K.G., and relating chiefly to manors in the counties of Norfolk and Suffolk', in HISTORICAL MANUSCRIPT COMMISSION *Report on manuscripts in various collections*, vol. VII. Cd.6722. H.M.S.O., 1914, 153-246.
REDSTONE, VINCENT B., ed. *Household book of Dame Alice de Bryene of Acton Hall, Suffolk, Sept. 1412—Sept. 1413.* Bungay: Suffolk Institute of Archaeology and History, 1984. Originally published 1931. Includes many names.

ECCLESIASTICAL ESTATES

Ecclesiastical estates were of great importance, especially prior to the Reformation. Their deeds were collected together into cartularies, many of which have been printed. These and other ecclesiastical estate records are listed here.
REDSTONE, V.B. 'Records of the Sudbury archdeaconry, pt.2', *S.I.A.* **11**, 1902, 267-300. Lists ecclesiastical terriers, i.e. surveys of church lands.

Blythburgh

HARPER-BILL, CHRISTOPHER, ed. *Blythburgh Priory cartulary.* 2 vols. Suffolk charters, **2-3**. Woodbridge: S.R.S., 1980-81.

Blythburgh *continued*
See also:
LYTE, H.C. MAXWELL. 'The manuscripts of the Rev. T.S. Hill', in HISTORICAL MANUSCRIPTS COMMISSION *Tenth report*, appendix, part IV. H.M.S.O., 1885, 451-7. Extracts from cartulary of Blythburgh Priory.

Bury St.Edmunds

THOMSON, RODNEY M, ed. *The archives of the abbey of Bury St.Edmunds.* S.R.S., **21**. Woodbridge: Boydell Press, 1980. Lists records held in various repositories.
DOUGLAS, D.C., ed. *Feudal documents from the abbey of Bury St.Edmunds.* Records of the social and economic history of England and Wales, **8**. Oxford University Press for the British Academy, 1932. Includes many deeds, 11-12th c.
DAVIS, R.H.C., ed. *The kalendar of Abbot Samson of Bury St.Edmunds and related documents.* Camden 3rd series, **84**. Royal Historical Society, 1954. Written between 1186 and 1191; includes surveys, etc., with many names. Also includes 165 charters of late 12th and early 13th c. date.
HALL, CATHERINE P. 'Three charters of Bury St.Edmunds Abbey in Corpus Christi College, Cambridge', *Archives* 15(65), 1981, 11-25. 12th c.
GRANSDEN, ANTONIA, ed. *The letter-book of William of Hoo sacrist of Bury St.Edmunds, 1280-1294.* S.R.S., **5**, 1963. Includes many names.
HERVEY, LORD FRANCIS, ed. *The Pinchbeck register relating to the Abbey of Bury St.Edmunds, etc.* 2 vols. Brighton: Farncombe's, 1925.
REDSTONE, LILIAN J. 'First ministers accounts of the possessions of the abbey of St.Edmund', *S.I.A.* **13**, 1909, 311-66. Account from the records of the Court of Augmentations, 1539-40, giving names of many tenants of former abbey property, mainly in Suffolk.

Butley

DICKENS, G., ed. *The register or chronicle of Butley Priory, Suffolk, 1510-1535.* Winchester: Warren & Son, 1951.
See also Leiston

Estate Papers continued
Ecclesiastical Estates continued

Clare

BARNARDISTON, K.W. *Clare Priory: seven centuries of a Suffolk house*. ed. Norman Scarfe. Cambridge: W. Heffer & Sons, 1962. Includes list of 198 deeds, with a list of priors, 1299-1535, and owners, 1248-1953, and chapters on the Frende, Barnardiston, Poulter and Barker families.

HARPER-BILL, C., ed. *The cartulary of the Augustinian Friars of Clare*. Suffolk charters, **11**. Woodbridge: S.R.S., 1991.

Eye

SCHOFIELD, B. 'The register of Eye priory', *British Museum Quarterly* **12**,1937-8, 9-10. Brief description of a cartulary.

Leiston

MORTIMER, RICHARD, ed. *Leiston Abbey cartulary and Butley Priory charters*. Suffolk charters, **1**. Ipswich: S.R.S., 1979.

SCHOFIELD, B. 'Wreck rolls of Leiston Abbey', in DAVIES, J.C., ed. *Studies presented to Sir Hilary Jenkinson*. Oxford: O.U.P., 1957, 361-71. Includes transcript of roll for 1505, giving many names.

Ramsey

AULT, WARREN ORTMAN, ed. *Court rolls of the abbey of Ramsey and of the Honor of Clare*. New Haven: Yale U.P.; London: Oxford U.P., 1928. 13th c. rolls of the honours of Broughton, Huntingdonshire, and Clare, Suffolk, the Banlieu of Ramsey Abbey, Huntingdonshire, and the Norfolk Hundred of Clackclose and Leet of Walsoken, etc.

Sibton

BROWN, PHILIPPA, ed. *Sibton Abbey cartularies and charters*. 4 vols. Suffolk charters, **7-10**. Woodbridge: S.R.S., 1985-88.

BROWN, R. ALLEN, ed. 'Early charters of Sibton Abbey, Suffolk', in BARNES, PATRICIA M., & SLADE, C.F., eds. *A medieval miscellany for Doris Mary Stenton*. Pipe Roll Society publications, **74**, 1962. Mostly 12th c.

DENNY, A.H., ed. *The Sibton Abbey estate: select documents, 1325-1509*. S.R.S., **2**,1960. Includes extent, 1325, rent rolls of 1328 and 1484 and accounts, 1363-4 and 1508-9.

Stoke by Clare

HARPER-BILL, CHRISTOPHER, & MORTIMER, RICHARD, eds. *Stoke by Clare cartulary: B.L. Cotton appx. xxi*. 3 vols. Suffolk charters, **4-5**. Woodbridge: S.R.S., 1982-4.

BY PLACE

Many estate records relating to particular places have been printed, and are listed here by place. Also listed here are manorial descents.

Aldeburgh

WINN, A.T. 'Lords of the manor of Aldeburgh, Suffolk', *E.A.M.* **1920**, 71 and 73. List.

Barking

L., H.R. 'Barking Manor, Suffolk', *E.A.M.* **1939**, 28-9, 31-2, 37, 41-2, 47 and 49. Abstracts of deeds.

Barsham

SUCKLING, F.H. 'Some notes on Barsham juxta Beccles, Co.Suffolk', *Genealogist* N.S. **21**, 1905, 124-42 and 243-50; **22**, 1906, 52-61, 128-34, 149-54 and 212-22; **23**, 1907, 11-18 and 73-9. See also **23**, 1907, 135-6. Includes wills, deeds, Chancery proceedings, etc., with notes on the medieval pedigrees of Eckingham, Lee and Suckling, and list of rectors.

Barton Mills

POWELL, EDGAR. 'Accounts and diary of Rev. John Rhodes, rector of Barton Mills, 1662-1667', *S.I.A.* **15**, 1915, 269-90. Accounts give many local names.

Bentley

P[ARTRIDGE], C. 'Bentley manorial rent roll of 1635', *E.A.M.* **1935**, 9-10, 12-13 and 14.

Brandon

MUNDAY, J.T. *Brandon manor rolls of the 1380's*. Lakenheath: J.T. Munday, 1972. Gives many names.

Bury St.Edmunds

REDSTONE, V.B. 'St.Edmund's Bury and town rental for 1295', *S.I.A.* **13**, 1909, 191-222. Rental of the Abbey's property in Bury St.Edmunds.

STATHAM, M.P. 'Bury St.Edmunds in 1433-1434', *Suffolk review* **4**(2), 1973, 7-15. Notes on a rental, with some names.

'Bury householders in 1527', *E.A.M.* **1908**, 109-10; 120-21 and 122-3. See also **1909**, 9. Rental of the Abbey, listing tenants.

Butley

WHITE, H.G.E. 'Unpublished fourteenth-century rent roll of the Priory of Butley, Suffolk, with singular liturgical, legal and other matter. ', *East Anglian* N.S. **11**, 1905-6, 1-6, 28-31, 45-6, 59-61, 72-3 and 87-8.

Cavendish

RUGGLES, T. 'Notices of the Manor of Cavendish in Suffolk and of the Cavendish family while possessed of that manor', *Archaeologia* **11**, 1794, 50-62. Includes pedigrees of Gernon and Cavendish, 14-16th c.

Clare

ARMSTEAD, J.B. 'Some account of the court leet of the borough of Clare, with extracts from the verdicts of the headboroughs', *S.I.A.* **2**, 1859, 103-12. Includes 17-18th c. extracts.

Cockfield

HERRIDGE, KEVIN. 'The secret drawer', *S.Rt.* **14**(3), 1988, 88-9. Lists names found in Cockfield Hall manorial court rolls, 1658-60.

Debenham

MORLEY, CLAUDE. 'The owners of Crows Hall in Debenham', *E.A.M.* **1921**, 75, 77, 78, 80, 82, 84 and 86. Descent.

Easton

PACKARD, JOHN. *Easton, Suffolk: the fields and field names*. London: the author, 1972. Includes list of land owners and occupiers in 1837.

Framlingham

RIDGARD, JOHN, ed. *Medieval Framlingham: select documents, 1270-1524*. S.R.S., **27**. Woodbridge: Boydell Press, 1985. Includes various 13-14th c. account rolls, a list of the household of Roger Bigod, the Earl Marshall, c.1294-5, etc., and records many names.

Framsden

M., S.M.W. 'A Framsden valuation, 1661', *E.A.M.* **1952**, 9-10, 12, 13-14 and 16. Survey, listing tenants.

Freckenham

CALLARD, ERNEST. *The manor of Freckenham, an ancient corner of East Anglia*. Bodley Head, 1924. Includes transcripts of medieval documents.

Hadleigh

HERVEY, LORD JOHN. 'Extent of Hadleigh manor, 1305', *S.I.A.* **11**, 1902, 152-72. Records names of many tenants.

Hepworth

CORBETT, W.J. & METHOLD, T. TINDAL. 'The rise and devolution of the manors in Hepworth, Suffolk', *S.I.A.* **10**, 1900, 19-48 and 125-43. Descent of the manors.

Herringswell

LIVETT, R.G.C. 'Some fourteenth century documents relating to Herringswell, Co.Suffolk', *East Anglian* N.S. **10**, 1903-4, 121-4, 253-5, 330-2, 386-9; **11**, 1905-6, 242-4, 269-71, 302-4 and 324-7. Terrier of lands the property of John Wysman, giving names of tenants; court rolls, etc.

Hollesley

NICHOLS, F.M. 'Court-roll of the manor of Hollesley, and the arms of Stanhope', *Proceedings of the Society of Antiquaries* 2nd series **3**, 1864-7, 260-64. Medieval-17th c.

Ickworth

COVELL, T. *Ickworth survey boocke. Ano 1665.* ed. J.H. Ipswich: [ ], 1893. Includes extract from will of John Hervey, 1556.

Ipswich

WEBB, JOHN. 'An Ipswich merchant's cloth accounts, 1623-24', *S.I.A.* **37**(2), 1990, 124-33. Includes names of clothiers and merchants mentioned in the accounts of Roger Cutler.

Ixworth

OLIVER, ANDREW. 'A rental of the manor of Ixworth, Suffolk', *East Anglian* N.S. **11**, 1905-6, 154-5. Rental of 1627.

Lakenheath

MUNDAY, J.T. *Lacy's land: documents*. Lakenheath records, **1**. Lakenheath: the author, 1969. Terrier of lands owned by Simeon Styward in 1533, formerly owned by John Lacy, giving many names.

Lawshall

SAUNDERS, H.W. 'A bailiff's roll of the manor of Lawshall, 1393-4', *S.I.A.* **14**, 1912, 111-46.

Layham

'Manor roll, Layham, 1338', *E.A.M.* **1916**, 67, 69, 71, 73 and 75.

Little Wratting

BLAKE, N.F. 'William Caxton and Suffolk', *S.I.A.* **29**, 1964, 139-53. See also **30**, 1967, 112-5. An edition of 17 deeds mainly concerned with Little Wratting, 15th c.

Little Wratting *continued*

SKEAT, T.C. 'The Caxton deeds', *British Museum Quarterly* **28**, 1964, 12-15. Lists deeds, 1420-67, relating mainly to Little Wratting.

Long Melford

HARRISON, ROGER. *Properties owners and tenants: a study of the East Side of Hall Street, Long Melford, Suffolk, 1441-1981*. Occasional publication, **2**. Long Melford: Long Melford Historical and Archaeological Society, 1989. Includes detailed notes on sources and many names.

Middleton Austins

WAYMAN, H.W. BILLING. 'Names and notes from the court book of the manor of Middleton Austins, co.Suffolk, 1694-1754', *East Anglian* N.S. **13**, 1909-10, 359-62.

Newmarket

MAY, PETER. *Court rolls of Newmarket in Suffolk, 1408-10*. Newmarket: the author, 1973.

Rattlesden

OLORENSHAW, J.R. 'Particulars of service in the manor of Rattlesden, from an extent of 1277', *East Anglian* N.S. **10**, 1903-4, 334-6, 353-4 and 370-72; **11**, 1905-6, 13-15 and 24-8.

Shipmeadow

S., F.H. 'Court rolls of Shipmeadow', *E.A.M.* **1915**, 39-60 and 63. 18th c.

Stoke by Nayland

TORLESSE, CHARLES MARTIN. *Some account of Stoke by Nayland, Suffolk*. Harrison & Sons, 1877. Descent of the manor, extracts from parish registers, and monumental inscriptions.

Stonham Aspall

CHAPMAN, DEREK. 'Ubbeston Hall in Stonham Aspall', *Suffolk review*, N.S. **4**(1), 1971, 46-52. Descent of property, 16-17th c.

Stuston

SMITH, LUCY TOULMIN, ed. *Common place book of the fifteenth century, containing a religious play and poetry, legal forms, and local accounts*. Privately printed, 1886. Includes rental for the East Common at Stuston, and a 'task book', undated, but c.15-16th c., many names.

Thorndon

'Thorndon: a 17th century rentall', *E.A.M.* **1928**, 6 and 7. Lists 1650 tenants.

Walpole

LEGG, MARJORIE. 'West House, Walpole, Suffolk: the history of a house', *Suffolk review*, N.S. **5**, 1985, 10-16.

Walsham le Willows

DODD, KENNETH MELTON, ed. *The field book of Walsham-le-Willows, 1577*. S.R.S., **17**, 1974. Gives names of tenants, etc.

Witnesham

'Witnesham, Suffolk', *E.A.M.* **1916**, 75-6. List of owners of the School House, 18-19th c.

Wykes

HUDSON, WILLIAM, ed. 'Three manorial extents of the thirteenth century', *Norfolk archaeology* **14**, 1899, 1-56. Relating to Bradcar and Barham in Norfolk, and Wykes, Suffolk.

15. RECORDS OF NATIONAL AND COUNTY ADMINISTRATION

Official lists of names, such as tax lists and muster rolls, have already been discussed. There are, however, many other records of central and local government which provide useful information. Publications relating to these records are listed here in rough chronological order.

GREEN, ANGELA. 'The stewardship of the liberty of the eight and a half hundreds', *S.I.A.* **30**, 1967, 255-62. i.e. West Suffolk. Lists some stewards and under-stewards, 11-19th c.

POTTER, GEORGE RICHARD, ed. *Translation of so much of the Pipe Roll of 31 Henry I as refers to Norfolk and Suffolk*. Rye's Norfolk handlists, series 2, no.2. Norwich: [ ], 1925.

HERVEY, LORD JOHN, ed. *The hundred rolls and extracts therefrom, made by authority, 2nd Edward I*. Ipswich: S. & W.J. King, 1902. Identifies tenants in chief, etc, Lothingland Hundred.

REDSTONE, V.B. 'Nomina villarum, Co.Suffolk, 1316', *S.I.A.* **11**, 1902, 173-99. Return of the names of lords of townships.

'Suffolk notes from the calendar of French rolls of the reign of Henry VI in the Public Records Office', *East Anglian* N.S. **13**, 1909-10, 105-8. List of men issued with 'protections'.

BULLEN, R. FREEMAN. 'Pardons for outlawry, 1399-1509', *E.A.M.* **1937**, 85-7; **1938**, 3, 4, 6, 7-8, 9-10, 11-12, 15, 17-18, 20, 24, 27, 30-31, 35, 37, 39, 40, 41-42, 44-45, 48, 50, 53 and 55. Gives many names.

'Suffolk witch trials: an index', *S.Rt.* **6**(3), 1980, 38-44. Lists 16-17th c. witches.

BULLEN, R. FREEMAN. 'Records of the Court of Star Chamber: Suffolk, temp. Henry VIII', *East Anglian* N.S. **13**, 1909-10, 233-6, 253-5, 269-72 and 294-5. List of Suffolk cases.

BULLEN, R. FREEMAN. 'Calendar of Exchequer depositions by commission during the reigns of Elizabeth and James I relating to the county of Suffolk', *S.I.A.* **14**, 1912, 9-56. Indexes plaintiffs and defendants in Exchequer law suits.

'Suffolk Chancery proceedings, temp. James I', *East Anglian* N.S. **4**, 1891-2, 120-22. Index, A-Bl only.

'Extracts from the Sessions Order Book, 1639-51', *S.I.A.* **15**, 1915, 162-82.

EVERITT, ALAN, ed. *Suffolk and the Great Rebellion, 1640-1660.* S.R.S., **3**, 1960. Includes original documents relating to the Parliamentarian county committees, etc., giving many names.

'Suffolk alehouses, 1712-14', *E.A.M.* **1936**, passim. List of licences granted.

CRISTIE, PETER. 'The sessions depositions', *S.Rt.* **10**(4), 1984, 85-8. See also **16**(4), 1991, 216-20. Lecture on Quarter sessions depositions, 1760-1820.

PEARSON, WILLIAM C. 'A Suffolk gaol calendar of the last century', *East Anglian* N.S. **4**, 1891-2, 113-4. 1787; lists prisoners.

PHILLIPS, J.S., ed. *Grand juries of Suffolk, 1800-80. The Judges of Assize and the High Sheriffs of the county* ... Bury St.Edmunds: E.L. Barker, 1882.

'Suffolk paupers', *S.Rt.* **7**(3), 1981, 40-41. List of paupers assisted to migrate to Lancashire and other northern counties, 1836.

BENTON, A. 'Index of Suffolk poor law migrants, 1836', *S.Rt.* **8**(3), 1982, 52-3; **8**(4), 1982, 72; **9**(1), 1983, 4; **9**(2), 1983, 34-5; **9**(3), 1983, 61-2. Gives names, ages, parishes of origin and destination, and number in families.

CHARITY COMMISSIONERS. *The charities in the county of Suffolk.* J. Coxhead, 1840. Includes information from many early reports, with extracts from wills, etc.

An account of the endowed charities in West Suffolk, prepared for the County Council. Ipswich: S. & W.J. King, 1895. Provides some information on trustees and wills, etc.

THOMAS, R.G. *A century of service: the county councils of Suffolk, 1889-1989.* Ipswich: Salient Press, 1989. Lists some 15,000 names of aldermen, councillors and chief officers.

16. RECORDS OF BOROUGH AND PAROCHIAL ADMINISTRATION

Parochial administration in the pre-industrial period resulted in the creation of a wide range of documents—churchwardens accounts, rate lists, overseers accounts, settlement examinations, deeds, tithe agreements, etc. It is unlikely that there were many whose names went totally unrecorded in these documents. For Suffolk, many extracts, calendars, etc., have been published, although much more remains in manuscript. Works dealing with parochial administration are listed here by parish.

Akenham

PEARSON, WILLIAM C. 'Entries relating to the tithe customs in the parish of Akenham', *East Anglian* N.S. **9**, 1901-2, 75-6; N.S. **11**, 1905-6, 37-8. Lists tithe due from some individuals, 1424.

Aldeburgh

WINN, ARTHUR T. 'Extracts from the Aldeburgh records', *Notes and queries* 12th series **7-9**, 1920-21, passim. Extracts from Chamberlains' account book, 1566-1649.

WINN, ARTHUR T. *Records of the borough of Aldeburgh: the Church.* Hertford: Stephen Austin, 1926. Includes many extracts from churchwardens' accounts, etc., with a list of vicars.

'Records of the Corporation of Aldeburgh in the county of Suffolk', in HISTORICAL MANUSCRIPTS COMMISSION *Report on manuscripts in various collections, vol.IV.* Cd.3218. H.M.S.O., 1907, 279-312.

Badley

P[ARTRIDGE], C. 'Badley's inhabitants in 1671, 1677, 1732-1743', *E.A.M.* **1926**, 46. Names from 'town booke' of principal inhabitants.

Bardwell

WARREN, F.E. 'Gild of S.Peter in Bardwell', *S.I.A.* **11**, 1902, 81-133. Guild, churchwardens', and town wardens' accounts, 16th c., giving many names.

Barnardiston

W., L.H.H. 'Barnardiston registers', *E.A.M.* **1932**,19-20, 21, 25, 27-8 and 38. Primarily a list of churchwardens and curates.

Beccles

ASHBY, W.J. 'Beccles churchwardens' accounts', *East Anglian* N.S. **2**, 1887-8, passim.

Beccles *continued*

ASHBY, W.J. 'Extracts from the Beccles overseers' account, 1637-1645', *East Anglian* N.S. **2**, 1887-8, 402-3.

MACRAY, W.D. 'Records of the corporation of Beccles, Suffolk', in HISTORICAL MANUSCRIPTS COMMISSION *Report on manuscripts in various collections, vol.VII.* Cd.6722. H.M.S.O., 1914, 70-79.

'Guild of the Holy Ghost, Beccles', *East Anglian*, N.S. **3**, 1869, 52-4, 91-2 and 116-21. Accounts, 17-18th c., with many names.

Bedingfield

MILLARD, J.W. 'Destruction of parish vermin in the sixteenth century at Bedingfield', *East Anglian* N.S. **2**, 1887-8, 328-9. Extracts from accounts, giving names.

Blything Union

An official account of the parochial charters and public trust funds belonging to each parish in the Blything Union. Halesworth: T. Tippell, 1838. Includes much information from wills and deeds, etc.

Boxford

NORTHEAST, PETER, ed. *Boxford churchwarden's accounts, 1530-1561.* S.R.S. **23**. Woodbridge: Boydell Press, 1982. Includes lists of rectors and churchwardens for the period covered.

Bradfield St.George

HASLEWOOD, FRANCIS. 'Bradfield S.George: army rate, 1649', *S.I.A.* **9**, 1897, 310. Rate list.

Bungay

BAKER, GRAY B. 'Extracts from churchwardens' books, no.4: Bungay, St.Mary, Suffolk', *East Anglian* **1**, 1863, 237-8, 375-7 and 423; **2**, 1866, 147-51, 227-30 and 275-8; **3**, 1869, 19-21, 43 and 198-200. 16th c.

Bury St.Edmunds

CHRISTIE, PETER. 'Oddments from the archives, 20', *S.Rt.* **8**(1), 1982, 3-4. Includes entries for Abbeygate Street from the rate book for St.Mary's parish, Bury St.Edmunds, 1794.

LOBEL, M.D. 'A list of the aldermen and bailiffs of Bury St.Edmunds from the twelfth to the sixteenth century', *S.I.A.* **22**,1936, 17-28.

REDSTONE, LILIAN J. *Records of the Guildhall feoffment deposited in the muniment room, Bury St.Edmunds (12th century—1939).* Bury: Free Press, 1940.

SYMONDS, WILLIAM. 'The booke of subscriptions, 1663-1705', *S.I.A.* **13**, 1909, 44-56. Oaths taken by officers and members of the corporation of Bury St.Edmunds.

Bury St.Edmunds

'The manuscripts of the corporation of Bury St.Edmunds', in HISTORICAL MANUSCRIPTS COMMISSION *Fourteenth report ...* C.7881. H.M.S.O., 1895, 121-58.

Clare

ARMSTEAD, J.B. *Extracts from the registers kept by the criers of Clare, Suffolk'*, East Anglian **1**, 1864, 384-6. Record of goods lost and found, with many local names.

Coddenham

L., W.M. 'Coddenham parish records', *E.A.M.* **1933**, passim. Includes extracts from various records, e.g. 1643 rate, giving many names.

Cratfield

HOLLAND, WILLIAM. *Cratfield: a transcript of the accounts of the parish, from A.D.1490 to A.D.1642 with notes.* ed. John James Raven. Jarrold & Sons, *1895*.

Dennington

RAVEN, J.J. 'Extracts from the parish book of Dennington, Co.Suffolk', *East Anglian* N.S. **3**, 1889-90, 273-4. 16th c.

Denston

HASLEWOOD, FRANCIS. 'Parish records of Denston', *S.I.A.* **6**, 1888, 425-32. Various documents, 17-19th c., giving many names.

Dunwich

MACRAY, W.D. 'Records of the dissolved Corporation of Dunwich', in HISTORICAL MANUSCRIPTS COMMISSION *Report on manuscripts in various collections, vol.VII.* Cd.6722. H.M.S.O., 1914, 80-113.

Elmsett

'Churchwardens book of Elmsett', *East Anglian* **1**, 1858-63, 66-8. Brief extracts, 1558-1663.

Eye

JEAFFRESON, JOHN CORDY. 'The manuscripts of the Corporation of Eye in the county of Suffolk', in HISTORICAL MANUSCRIPTS COMMISSION *Tenth report,* appendix, part IV. H.M.S.O., 1885, 513-36.

Haughley

MACCULLOUGH, NIGEL. 'Churchwardens' accounts of St.Mary-the-Virgin, Haughley, 1664-83', *Suffolk review* **3**, 1970, 273-85. General discussion with some extracts.

Haverhill

MIZON, LIONEL. 'The Haverhill parish constables, 1790-1809', *Haverhill Historian* **11**(1), 1982, 3-8.

Henley

PEARSON, W.C. 'Extracts from the churchwardens' and overseers' accounts of the parish of Henley, Suffolk, commencing 1602', *East Anglian* N.S. **4**, 1891-2, 92-4.

Heveningham

P[ARTRIDGE], C. 'Heveningham's registers', *E.A.M.* **1931**, 45. List of various parochial records bound with the registers.

Ipswich

BACON, NATHLL. *The annalls of Ipswiche ...* ed. William H. Richardson. Ipswich: S.H. Cowell, 1884. Extracts from town records pre-1654, with many names.

CANNING, RICHARD. *Account of the gifts and legacies that have been given and bequethed to charitable uses in the town of Ipswich ...* New ed. Ipswich: Dorkin, 1819. Includes notes on wills, deeds, trustees, etc.

CHAMBERLAIN, HERBERT, ed. *Ipswich 200 years ago: showing the extent and rateable value of the town at that period; being a correct copy of an assessment made in the year 1689 ...* Ipswich: East Anglian Daily Times, [1889].

CROSS, R.L. *Justice in Ipswich, 1200-1968.* Ipswich: Ipswich Corporation, 1968. Detailed discussion of the history of justice; useful background, but little of direct genealogical interest.

FITCH, W.S. 'Notices of the Corpus Christi Guild, Ipswich', *S.I.A.* **2**, 1859, 151-63. Includes extracts from original documents, 15-17th c., giving names of officers, etc.

GRIMSEY, B.P. *The Freemen of the borough of Ipswich.* Ipswich: privately printed, 1892. Includes lists, 18-19th c., etc., with biographical notes.

HUTCHINSON, M.B. 'Ipswich apprentice books', *Notes and queries,* 10th Series **1**, 1904, 41-2. See also 111. Description of Ipswich apprenticeship records, 16-17th c.

LAYTON, W.E. 'Notices from the Great Court and Assembly Books of the borough of Ipswich', *East Anglian,* N.S. **1-8**, 1885/6-1899/1900, passim. Includes many items omitted by Bacon.

LAYTON, W.E. 'The "taske book" of St.Mary at the Tower, Ipswich, 7 James I', *East Anglian* N.S. **1**, 1885-6, 217-21. Parochial assessment, giving many names.

Ipswich *continued*

MARTIN, G.H. *The early court rolls of the Borough of Ipswich*. Department of English Local History, occasional paper, **5**. Leicester: University College of Leicester, 1954. Analysis of the court rolls to 1334, with a list.

MARTIN, G.H., ed. *The Ipswich recognizance rolls, 1294-1327: a calendar*. S.R.S., **16**, 1973. Records conveyances of burgage tenements, and proofs of testaments in the borough court.

MARTIN, GEOFFREY H. 'The records of the Borough of Ipswich to 1422', *Journal of the Society of Archivists* **1**(4), 1956, 87-93.

WEBB, JOHN. 'The Ipswich deposition books, 1572-1607', *Suffolk review* **2**, 1959, 22-6. Brief description.

WEBB, JOHN. 'Elizabethan piracy: the evidence of the Ipswich Deposition Books', *Suffolk review* **2**, 1961, 59-65. Brief discussion.

WEBB, JOHN, ed. *Poor relief in Elizabethan Ipswich*. S.R.S., **9**, 1966. Includes names of many poor, including a census of the poor, 1597 and a poor rate assessment 1574.

'The account books of Christ's Hospital, Ipswich', *East Anglian* N.S. **1**, 1885-6, 336-9. Accounts of an almshouse, 16-17th c., with many names.

'Extracts from the churchwardens' books of St.Clement's, Ipswich, A.D.1594-1652', *East Anglian* N.S. **3**, 1889-90, 203-6, 289-91 and 355-7; N.S. **4**, 1891-2, 4-7.

'Extracts from the churchwardens' books of accounts, St.Matthews, Ipswich, A.D.1574-1676', *East Anglian* N.S. **4**, 1891-2, 102-3, 122-6, 134-6, 155-7, 172-3 and 343-5.

'The manuscripts of the Corporation of Ipswich, Co.Suffolk', in HISTORICAL MANUSCRIPTS COMMISSION *Ninth report ...* C.3773. H.M.S.O., 1883, 222-62.

Layham

'Layham rate-payers, 1771', *E.A.M.* **1937**, 62. List.

Linstead Parva

BAKER, GRAY B. 'Extracts from churchwardens' books, no.8: Linstead Parva, Suffolk', *East Anglian* **2**, 1866, 48-9 and 128-9. 1639 and 1765-86.

Little Cornard

DEEDES, CECIL. 'Old documents belonging to the parish of Little Cornard', *East Anglian* N.S. **1**, 1885-6, passim. See also N.S. **3**, 1889-90, 73-7. Extracts from various documents in the parish chest, giving many names.

Long Melford

DEEDES, CECIL. 'Dr. Bisbie's manuscript collections for Long Melford', *S.I.A.* **7**, 1891, 78-90. Primarily the rectors tithe accounts, 17th c.

DYMOND, DAVID & PAINE, CLIVE. *The spoil of Melford church: the reformation in a Suffolk parish*. Ipswich: Salient Press, 1989. Includes original sources with brief biographical notes on local people.

'Melford parish poor rate, 1758', *E.A.M.* **1944**, passim.

Lowestoft

LEES, HUGH D.W. *The chronicles of a Suffolk parish church: Lowestoft St.Margaret*. Lowestoft: [ ], 1949. Includes extracts from parish registers, lists of parish officers, monumental inscriptions, etc.

Mellis

CREED, HENRY. 'Extracts from the accompts of the churchwardens of Mellis from A.D.1611 to A.D.1645', *Proceedings of the Bury and West Suffolk Archaeological Institute* **1**, 1853, 79-83.

Mendlesham

JEAFFRESON, JOHN CORDY. 'The manuscripts of the parish of Mendlesham, Co.Suffolk', in HISTORICAL MANUSCRIPTS COMMISSION *Fifth report of the Royal Commission on Historical Manuscripts, Pt.1*. Cd.1432. H.M.S.O., 1876, 593-6. Includes will of Henry Jesop, 1516.

Metfield

BOWER, NORAH M. 'Extracts from Metfield churchwardens' account books and from loose bills in the church chest', *S.I.A.* **23**, 1939, 128-47. 16-17th c.

Mildenhall

'Extracts from churchwardens' books, 2: Mildenhall, Suffolk', *East Anglian* **1**, 1858-63, 185-7 and 198-9.

Nayland

'Nayland workhouse', *S.Rt.* **15**(2), 1989, 54-5. Includes list of inmates, 1749.

North Cove

X. 'Extracts from churchwardens' books, no.13: North Cove, Suffolk', *East Anglian* 2, 1866, 328-9. 18th c.

Orford

MACRAY, W.D. 'Records of the dissolved Corporation of Orford, Suffolk', in HISTORICAL MANUSCRIPTS COMMISSION *Report on manuscripts in various collections, vol.IV.* Cd.3218. H.M.S.O., 1907, 255-78. Includes various wills, deeds, etc.

Southwold

BRADLEY, S. 'Bailiffs of Southwold', *S.Rt.* 4(4), 1978, 55; 5(1), 1979, 11; 5(2), 1979, 31. List, 1490-1800.

MACRAY, W.D. 'The records of Southwold, Suffolk', in HISTORICAL MANUSCRIPTS COMMISSION *Report on manuscripts in various collections,* vol.VII. Cd.6722. H.M.S.O., 1914, 114-8.

'Southwold records', *E.A.M.* **1936**, passim. 18-19th c. extracts from overseers' accounts, etc., lists many names.

Stowmarket

HARPER, A.C. 'Subscriptions to poor charity, borowghe of Stowmarket, 20 April 1610-20 April 1611', *S.Rt.* 3(1), 1977, 53. List of some 45 names.

Sudbury

BERRY, ALLAN. *A book conteyning the names of the free burgesses of the Burrough of Sudbury ... (1703).* Colchester: the author, 1978. Lists 731 names.

BERRY, ALLAN, ed. *Admissions to the freedom of the borough of Sudbury.* 3 vols. Colchester: the author, 1986-8.

BRAITHWAITE, T.M., ed. *Sudbury common lands: a synopsis of the title deeds relating to the lands administered by the Common Land Trustees on behalf of the freemen of the Borough of Sudbury, Suffolk.* [Sudbury]: [the trustees], 1911.

Sudbury *continued*

STOKES, ETHEL & REDSTONE, LILIAN. 'Calendar of the muniments of the borough of Sudbury', *S.I.A.* **13**, 1909, 259-310b.

Tuddenham St.Mary

W., L.H.H. 'Tuddenham St.Mary register', *E.A.M.* **1932**, 35 and 36-7. Primarily a list of churchwardens, 17-18th c.

Walberswick

BULLEN, R. FREEMAN. 'Walberswick in 1628', *E.A.M.* **1917**, 108 and 112. Poor rate, giving names.

LEWIS, R.W.M., ed. *Walberswick churchwardens' accounts, A.D.1450-1499.* Headley Bros, 1947.

Weybread

CALVER, JOHN. 'Extracts from churchwardens' books, no.5: Weybread, Suffolk, 1587-1738', *East Anglian* 1, 1863, 409-11; 2, 1866, 4-6 and 34-7.

Witnesham

M., S.M.W. 'A Witnesham rate in 1644', *E.A.M.* **1943**, 21-2, 23, 25 and 26.

Woodbridge

The terrier of Woodbridge ... to which are added the principal donations at large extracted from wills, deeds, etc., with notes and explanations. 2nd ed. R. Baldwin, 1811. Includes a few monumental inscriptions, etc.

Yaxley

JEAFFRESON, JOHN CORDY. 'The manuscripts of the Reverend William Henry Sewell, M.A., vicar of Yaxley, Suffolk', in HISTORICAL MANUSCRIPTS COMMISSION *Tenth report,* appendix, part IV. H.M.S.O., 1885, 463-6. Deeds, etc., presumably from the parish chest.

17. EDUCATIONAL RECORDS

Educational records can provide the genealogist with much useful information. For Suffolk, a number of school registers and other lists of staff and pupils have been published:

Bungay

[HOUGHTON, R.R.] *Bungay Grammar School, 1565-1965*. Bungay: [ ], 1965. Includes names of many staff and some boys.

Bury St.Edmunds

H[ERVEY], S.H.A. *Biographical list of boys educated at King Edward VI Free Grammar School, Bury St.Edmunds, from 1550 to 1900*. S.G.B. **13**. Bury St.Edmunds: Paul & Mathew, 1908.

Bury St.Edmunds' Grammar school list, 1900-1925. Bury St.Edmunds: [the School], 1930.

Culford

WATSON, F.E. *Culford School: the first hundred years, 1881-1981*. Culford: Culford School, 1980. Lists many staff and students.

Framlingham

Framlingham College register. 4th ed. [Framlingham]: Society of Old Framlinghamians, 1968.

Ipswich

GRAY, I.E. & POTTER, W.E. *Ipswich school, 1400-1950*. Ipswich: W.E. Harrison & Sons, 1950. Appendices include lists of headmasters, ushers (i.e. second masters), benefactors, and various others connected with the school.

MORFEY, W.M. *Ipswich School: an alphabetical list of Ipswichians known to have been educated at the school ... to ... 1857*. Ipswich: [the School?], 1976. Gives parentage.

STONE, H. 'The Ipswich charity schools of Grey Coat boys and Blue Coat girls', *S.I.A.* **25**, 1952, 172-92. Includes appendix listing teachers.

Woodbridge

[CRISP, F.A., ed.] *Liber admissionum: Seckford Grammar School at Woodbridge*. Suffolk: F.A. Crisp, 1900.

Woodbridge *continued*

'Woodbridge scholars', *East Anglian* **4**, 1870, 97-103. List of Woodbridge Grammar School admissions, 1670-1889.

Strays

Suffolk pupils who attended schools in other counties are listed in:

Ackworth

BULLEN, R. FREEMAN. 'Suffolk children at Ackworth (Quakers) School, 1779-1831', *E.A.M.* **1925**, 76, 80 and 88; 1926, 74 and 48. Ackworth, Yorkshire.

Merchant Taylors

BULLEN, R. FREEMAN. 'Suffolk boys at Merchant Taylors School, London, 1562 to 1699', *E.A.M.* **1917**, 34-5 and 36-7.

Colchester

'Suffolk boys at Colchester Grammar School, 1637-1737', *E.A.M.* **1916**, 58, 60, 62-3 and 65. List of boys.

Suffolk matriculands at a Cambridge college are listed in:

VENN, JOHN. 'The matriculation or admission books of Gonville and Caius College, Cambridge: East Anglian admissions from 1560', *East Anglian* N.S. **1-2**, 1885/6-1887/8, passim.

Other works which may be of use include:

IMRAY, J.M. 'Scholarships awarded by the Technical Instruction Committee of the East Suffolk County Council, 1893-1903', *Suffolk review* **3**, 1965-70, 18-24. Includes list of scholars, with residences and parents occupation, etc.

NORTHEAST, PETER. 'The charity school movement in Suffolk: evidence from the records of the S.P.C.K.', *Suffolk review*, N.S. **14**, 1990, 1-29. Includes brief information on Suffolk correspondents of the society, 18th c.

18. MIGRATION

Many emigrants from Suffolk have settled in far distant lands. In order to trace them, you need access to records held both in England, and in the places where they settled. It is not my purpose here to give a full listing of works on Suffolk emigrants. The following is merely a select list of publications I have come across which may prove useful to the genealogist. Further assistance may be had from the works listed in chapter 16 of my *English genealogy: an introductory bibliography*.

North America

East Anglians were an important contingent in the puritan migration to New England; John Winthrop, one of the leaders, was a Suffolk man. See:

BANKS, CHARLES EDWARD. *The Winthrop fleet of 1630: an account of the vessels, the voyage, the passengers and their English homes, from original authorities*. Boston: Houghton Mufflin, 1930. Includes biographical notes on passengers, who came from 20 different counties, but mainly Suffolk, Essex and London.

See also:

FLOWERDEN, R. 'Suffolk emigrants to New England, 1620-1650', *S.Rt.* **9**(4), 1983, 77-82. List, giving places of origin and destination.

BARTLETT, J.G. 'New England colonists from Rattlesden, co.Suffolk, England', *New England historical and genealogical register* **57**, 1903, 331-2. Brief note with names.

HARRIS, JOHN RYDEN. *East Anglia and America*. Ipswich: East Anglian Magazine, 1973. Includes list of 85 Suffolk emigrants.

Poverty, rather than religion, was an important motive for emigration in the nineteenth century. The names and ages of 35 persons who were assisted to emigrate from Fressingfield are given in:

RAVEN, JOHN. 'Families in Fressingfield, England, 1836, wishing to emigrate to America', *New England historical and genealogical register* **49**, 1895, 337-8.

Australia and New Zealand

The motive behind emigration to Australia in the early nineteenth century was neither religion, nor poverty. The original colonies were established for the punishment of crime—and many Suffolk convicts found themselves sentenced to transportation. A number of lists have been published in *Suffolk roots*—although it must be remembered that sentences of transportation were not always executed.

Australia and New Zealand *continued*

CORNELL, RICHARD. 'Criminal registers, 1791-1868', *S.Rt.* **14**(3), 1988, 84-6. Lists Suffolk men sentenced to transportation, 1820-22.

SMITH, L.F. 'Transportees from the Beccles gaol books, 1819-1847', *S.Rt.* **14**(4), 1988, 130-32.

'Woodbridge gaol books: transportees, 1825-1840', *S.Rt.* **14**(2), 1988, 44-5. Gives names, ages, crime, sentence, locality and year.

'More convicts from Suffolk sentenced to transportation', *S.Rt.* **15**(1), 1989, 25.

BENTON, A. 'Parish assisted emigrants from Suffolk, 1836', *S.Rt.* **13**(3), 1987, 67-8; **14**(1), 1988, 11-12; **14**(2), 1988, 40. Gives names, ages and parishes.

SMITH, L. 'Index to prisoners held in Ipswich (county) gaol and sentenced to transportation, 1840-1862', *S.Rt.* **13**(4), 1987, 98-9; **14**(1), 1988, 14-15. Gives ages, birthplaces, year, sentence, crime and place committed.

'Convicts transported to Van Diemans Land in 1844: all from Suffolk courts', *S.Rt.* **10**(4), 1984, 78-80.

SMITH, G. 'Some Suffolk emigrants on ships to Canterbury, New Zealand', *S.Rt.* **15**(4), 1989, 192-3.

See also:

DEEKS, RICHARD. *Those transported from Glemsford to Australia, 1787-1868*. The author, 1987. Lists 38 names, giving details of offence, trial and journey.

Immigrants

Suffolk has also attracted immigrants from the continent. A number of brief notes concerning these have been published:

BULLEN, R. FREEMAN. 'Suffolk aliens naturalised in 1436', *E.A.M.* **1920**, 72, 74, 75-6, 77, 80 and 82.

REDSTONE, V.B. 'Surnames: aliens in Bury in 1485', *E.A.M.* **1935**, 50. List of aliens.

REDSTONE, V.B. 'Alien settlers in Ipswich in 1485', *E.A.M.* **1937**, 16, 17 and 19.

REDSTONE, VINCENT B. 'The Dutch and Huguenot settlements of Ipswich', *Proceedings of the Huguenot Society of London* **12**, 1917-23, 183-204. Includes lists of names, 1568, 1576, 1695 and 1711.

'French Protestant refugees at Ipswich in connection with the linen industry during the seventeenth century', *East Anglian* N.S. **2**, 1887-8, 374-9 and 398-400. Accounts, gives many names.

FAMILY NAME INDEX

80

PLACE NAME INDEX

AUTHOR INDEX